Unprotected

How the normalisation of underage sex is exposing children and young people to the risk of sexual exploitation

Norman Wells

FAMILY EDUCATION TRUST

FAMILY EDUCATION TRUST
First published 2017

ISBN 978-0-906229-24-8

Family Education Trust
The Atrium
31 Church Road
Ashford
Middlesex
TW15 2UD

email: info@familyeducationtrust.org.uk
website: www.familyeducationtrust.org.uk

Family Education Trust is a company limited by guarantee (No 3503533) and a registered charity (No 1070500).

Printed in Great Britain by Newnorth Print, Bedford
Cover image credit: Klahan/Shutterstock

CONTENTS

PART 3 – CONCLUSION AND RECOMMENDATIONS

FOREWORD

The appalling revelations of systematic child abuse and exploitation in English towns and cities over the past few years have led to a considerable amount of soul-searching about the root causes of the crisis. In this report, Norman Wells draws attention to a neglected but critical aspect of the debate. He has drawn together the findings of a series of serious case reviews and an independent inquiry looking at the reasons why the abuse of so many young people was not picked up by professionals.

The report is utterly damning. A clear picture emerges of a culture in which underage sexual activity has come to be viewed as a normal part of growing up and seen as relatively harmless as long as it is consensual. Combined with official policies to encourage the confidential provision of contraception to minors, it becomes clear that current approaches aimed at improving teenage sexual health have frequently facilitated and perpetuated the sexual abuse of vulnerable young people.

At the heart of the problem has been the apparent tension that professionals working in the field of adolescent sexual health have faced between protecting young people from abuse and trying to reduce the likelihood of underage pregnancy. The serious case reviews reviewed in this report make it clear that too many professionals have focused on the latter at the expense of the former. In case after case, the sexual abuse of young people has been facilitated by the willingness of agencies to provide minors with birth control with very few questions being asked. At the same time, an unhealthy emphasis on confidentiality has been used too often as an excuse to exclude parents who might have been in a position to help stop the abuse at an earlier stage.

The 2015 Oxfordshire case review identifies the heart of the problem succinctly: '…a child may be judged mature enough to get contraceptives to have sex with an adult at an age when they are deemed in law unable to give consent to the sex itself' (see p. 43). To read how this contradiction has affected real children is heart-breaking.

It is impossible not to be angered by the case of 'Julia' in Thurrock who was abused over a number of years from the age of 12. The only response of her GP and the school sexual health drop-in service was to provide her with contraception. 'Child F' was a vulnerable 15 year-old with special needs from Hampshire who was being sexually abused at school. Because the school judged her to be engaging in consensual sexual activity, her parents were not informed and, as a result, 'Child F' continued to suffer abuse for years.

Ironically, the statistical evidence suggests there is actually no tension between sexual health outcomes and protecting children. Peer-reviewed research generally finds that the confidential provision of contraception to minors does not reduce conception or abortion rates. Indeed, a number of studies have found that easier access to emergency birth control for adolescents has contributed to the rise in sexually transmitted infections amongst teenagers. There really is no excuse for any health professional not to prioritise child protection above everything else when evidence comes to light that a minor is engaging in sexual activity.

Despite the fact that several of the serious case reviews have called for the government to revisit policy in this area, there is little evidence that lessons have been learned. Indeed, recent calls to tackle abuse by forcing schools to provide compulsory sex education lessons on 'consent' completely ignore the evidence that it is the over-emphasis on consent as a necessary and sufficient condition for underage sex which has been a contributing factor to the exploitation of young people.

Astonishingly, the government has recently endorsed the use of the Brook Sexual Behaviours Traffic Light resource for identifying sexual abuse. As the report reveals, the traffic light tool instructs schools to view sexual activity between minors aged 13 and over as a 'positive choice' as long as it is consensual. It is as if Rotherham, Rochdale and Oxfordshire had never happened. Quite rightly, Norman Wells calls for the Brook safeguarding tool to be withdrawn as a matter of urgency.

With the publication of this report, policymakers and professionals working in sexual health no longer have any excuse to ignore the evidence. The report makes a number of sensible recommendations to improve the way in which professionals deal with underage sexual activity and confidentiality. It is of the utmost importance that the government takes the findings of this report seriously and undertakes an urgent review of its approach to confidential sexual health services.

Professor David Paton
Nottingham University Business School

EXECUTIVE SUMMARY

The evidence

- High levels of child sexual exploitation – including child-on-child sexual exploitation – have been the subject of growing concern over recent years and the government has proposed a comprehensive response involving healthcare, social care, education, law enforcement, the voluntary sector, and local and national government.
- A study of recent serious case reviews and the Independent Inquiry into Child Sexual Exploitation in Rotherham reveals fundamental flaws in professional attitudes towards children and young people and towards underage sexual activity. The evidence shows:
  - — a complacent attitude towards underage sexual activity, with the assumption that, in the absence of any significant age disparity, it is consensual and a normal part of growing up;
  - — a professional readiness to routinely provide contraception to young people under the legal age of consent in confidence, without considering the possibility that they may be suffering abuse;
  - — a tendency to dismiss the concerns of parents;
  - — an inclination to treat children under the age of 16 as adults with the competence to make their own decisions with regard to sexual activity.

How public policy is placing children and young people at risk

The age of consent

- A tendency on the part of the authorities to turn a blind eye towards sexual activity below the age of 16, provided it is believed to be consensual and the parties are of a similar age, is leaving young teenage girls vulnerable to approaches from predatory males.
- Not only is there a reluctance to initiate criminal proceedings for sexual activity below the age of 16 when it is deemed to be consensual,

but there is also a disinclination to view it as a safeguarding issue.

- Crown Prosecution Service guidance allows for the possibility of consensual sexual activity involving children under the age of 13.
- The evidence suggests that a relaxed attitude towards the legal age of consent has contributed to a rise in the incidence of underage sex and of cases of child sexual exploitation.

Confidentiality policies

- The serious case reviews raise major questions about the common presumption that confidentiality policies are serving the best interests of children and young people.
- With its emphasis on the duty of confidentiality, Department of Health guidance on contraceptive and sexual and reproductive health services for under-16s gives the impression that young people are free to make an 'informed choice' to engage in unlawful sexual activity below the age of 16.
- There is both anecdotal and academic evidence to show that the confidential provision of contraception to under-16s has facilitated rather than hindered sexual experimentation among children and young people.
- Confusion over guidance on patient confidentiality is undermining child safeguarding procedures and placing vulnerable children and young people at risk of sexual exploitation.
- General Medical Council guidance for doctors on confidentiality recognises that there can be a conflict between confidentiality and child protection, but still insists that children under the age of 16 who are deemed to be of sufficient maturity are entitled to confidential contraception, abortion and sexual health services. The guidance even falls short of advocating the mandatory reporting on sexually active children below the age of 13.
- Government guidance to school nurses is also contributing to the normalisation of unlawful sex under the age of 16 and exposing children and young people to increased risk of sexual exploitation and abuse.

Sex and relationships education

- Evidence from the serious case reviews suggests that a relativistic approach to sex and relationships education does not hold the solution to keeping children and young people safe, but it is rather part of the problem. The moral confusion that has resulted from an abandonment of moral absolutes is placing children and young people at risk.
- Children and young people are being exposed to increased risk of sexual exploitation through messages commonly taught in sex and relationships education to the effect that sexual expression is a means to self-gratification and pleasure, and that young people must be free to decide for themselves 'when they are ready' for sex.
- 'Comprehensive sex and relationships education' has created in young people the expectation that they will have a series of casual sexual relationships. Within this culture, sexual exploitation has been allowed to go undetected and vulnerable young people have been deprived of protection.
- By reducing sexual safety and responsibility to the use of contraception and the giving and receiving of consent, sex education lessons in many schools are exposing children and young people to increased risk of sexual exploitation.

The sexual 'rights' of children and young people

- The notion that children and young people have sexual 'rights' is undermining both the responsibility of parents for the care and protection of their children and the basic principles of safeguarding.

The Brook Sexual Behaviours Traffic Light Tool

- The use of the Brook Sexual Behaviours Traffic Light Tool is calculated to further encourage a climate in which underage sex is viewed as a normal part of growing up. By giving 'positive feedback' to young people deemed to be in consensual sexual relationships below the age of 16, professionals may inadvertently be condoning and promoting sexual exploitation and abuse.

Conclusion

- Even though the serious case reviews and independent inquiry in Rotherham have repeatedly identified the normalisation of underage sex as a major reason for the complacency of child protection agencies, the government has given no indication that it has any plans to address the issue.
- The evidence demonstrates that a review of professional attitudes towards underage sexual activity and an investigation into the unintended consequences of teenage pregnancy strategies that have a focus on sex education and confidential contraceptive services are long overdue.
- The problem of child sexual exploitation is not primarily systemic, but social, cultural and moral. It will therefore not be resolved by restructuring and improved communications within local authority and police departments.
- There needs to be a fundamental change in how children and young people are treated, how parental responsibility is understood, how the family unit is regarded, and how the law is administered.

Introduction

Over the past five years, a series of serious case reviews has revealed the way in which attitudes towards underage sexual activity and policies in relation to the provision of contraception to minors have contributed to the sexual abuse and exploitation of children. In this report, we bring together for the first time the findings of seven serious case reviews concerned with child sexual exploitation (CSE) and of the independent inquiry into child sexual exploitation in Rotherham.

High levels of child sexual exploitation have been the subject of mounting concern over recent years. The British public has been horrified by the nature and scale of the exploitation and abuse perpetrated against girls and young women set out in well-publicised serious case reviews from Rochdale and Oxfordshire, and in the review of child sexual exploitation in Rotherham. In its National Strategic Assessment of Serious and Organised Crime for 2016, the National Crime Agency listed child sexual exploitation and abuse as one of the top five threats to the UK.[1]

In March 2015, the then Home Secretary Theresa May gave child sexual abuse the status of a national threat in the Strategic Policing Requirement (SPR) in order to ensure that it is prioritised by every police force. The revised edition of the SPR stated that, while not a threat to national security as identified in the National Security Strategy, child sexual abuse remained 'a threat of national importance'. The document continued: 'Its potential magnitude and impact necessitate a cohesive, consistent, national effort to ensure police and partners can safeguard children from harm.'[2]

At the same time, in direct response to Professor Alexis Jay's review of child sexual exploitation in Rotherham, the government announced the creation of a step change in its response and highlighted a number of measures that it would be taking. Among these measures was to make child sexual exploitation 'a priority for providers of health services'.[3] There can be no denying that the government is taking the issue with the utmost seriousness.

1 National Crime Agency, *National Strategic Assessment of Serious and Organised Crime 2016*, 9 September 2016, p.3.

2 Home Office, *The Strategic Policing Requirement*, March 2015, pp.7-8.

3 HM Government, *Tackling Child Sexual Exploitation*, March 2015, p.10.

Definitions

Child sexual exploitation has been variously defined. Two of the most commonly-used definitions have been those found in the supplementary guidance to *Working Together to Safeguard Children* issued in 2009[4] and in the non-statutory guidance for practitioners, *What to do if you're worried a child is being abused*, issued in 2015.[5] However, after a public consultation exercise, the government published a revised definition in February 2017:

> Child sexual exploitation is a form of child sexual abuse. It occurs where an individual or group takes advantage of an imbalance of power to coerce, manipulate or deceive a child or young person under the age of 18 into sexual activity (a) in exchange for something the victim needs or wants, and/or (b) for the financial advantage or increased status of the perpetrator or facilitator. The victim may have been sexually exploited even if the sexual activity appears consensual. Child sexual exploitation does not always involve physical contact; it can also occur through the use of technology.[6]

In its consultation paper on the statutory definition of *child sexual exploitation*, the government indicated that the current definition of child sexual abuse as found in *Working Together to Safeguard Children* will remain unchanged:

> [Sexual abuse] involves forcing or enticing a child or young person to take part in sexual activities, not necessarily involving a high level of violence, whether or not the child is aware of what is happening. The activities may involve physical contact, including assault by penetration (for example, rape or oral sex) or non-penetrative acts such as masturbation, kissing, rubbing and touching outside of clothing. They may also include non-contact activities, such as involving children in looking at, or in the production of, sexual images, watching sexual activities, encouraging children to behave in sexually inappropriate ways, or grooming a child in preparation for abuse (including via the internet). Sexual abuse is not solely perpetrated by adult males. Women can also commit acts of sexual abuse, as can other children.[7]

4 Department for Children, Schools and Families, *Safeguarding Children and Young People from Sexual Exploitation*, August 2009, p.9.

5 HM Government, *What to do if you're worried a child is being abused*, March 2015, p.9.

6 HM Government, *Definition of child sexual exploitation: Government consultation response*, 16 February 2017, p.3.

7 HM Government, *Statutory definition of child sexual exploitation: Government consultation*, 12 February 2016, p.8. The definition of child sexual abuse will be found in: HM Government, *Working Together to Safeguard Children*, March 2015, p.93.

Peer-on-peer abuse

It is a common perception that the perpetrators of child sexual exploitation and sexual abuse are invariably adults. Responses to freedom of information requests sent by the NSPCC to all police forces in England and Wales revealed that 4,209 young people under the age of 18 were recorded as the perpetrators of sexual offences against other children in 2013-14.[8] More recent figures obtained by Barnardo's suggest that recorded cases of children committing sexual offences against other children rose by 78 per cent between 2013 and 2016.[9]

Chief Constable Simon Bailey, the National Police Chiefs' Council Lead for Child Protection Abuse Investigation, told a parliamentary inquiry that:

> When you break down the profile of investigations and where abuse is taking place…we can say that around 30 per cent is peer-on-peer abuse… The most prolific [form of CSE] is peer-on-peer abuse being conducted by people younger than 18 years of age. When you look at core statistics you can see that 20 per cent of offenders charged with CSE offences are under the age of 18.[10]

The Local Government Association therefore reports that it is a myth that child sexual exploitation always involves the abuse of children by adults. In reality, it states:

> Peer-on-peer child sexual exploitation happens too and this can take various different forms. For example, young people are sometimes used to 'recruit' others, by inviting them to locations for parties where they will then be introduced to adults or forced to perform sexual acts on adults. Technology can also play a significant role, with young people known to use mobile technology as a way of distributing images of abuse.[11]

The government's response to date

In its report on *Tackling Child Sexual Exploitation*, the government insisted that a piecemeal approach was insufficient to address what it describes as an 'appalling crime' and a serious, national threat. The action plan states:

8 NSPCC, Harmful sexual behaviour: Facts and statistics *https://www.nspcc.org.uk/preventing-abuse/child-abuse-and-neglect/harmful-sexual-behaviour/harmful-sexual-behaviour-facts-statistics/* Accessed 22 February 2017.

9 Barnardo's 'Police figures reveal rise of almost 80% in reports of child-on-child sex offences', 3 February 2017.

10 Nusrat Ghani (chair), *Now I know it was wrong: Report of the parliamentary inquiry into support and sanctions for children who display harmful sexual behaviour*, Barnardo's, 2016, p.14.

11 Local Government Association, *Tackling child sexual exploitation: A resource pack for councils*, December 2014, p.18.

> Our response needs to be comprehensive. It needs to bring together healthcare, social care, education, law enforcement, the voluntary sector, local and national government. No one part of the system can tackle this on its own, and we cannot be complacent about progress. We will continue to keep the structure and the system as a whole under review.[12]

The report proposes a range of measures aimed at:

- strengthening the accountability of professionals responsible for child protection;
- changing the culture of denial and improving the early identification and reporting of concerns by professionals and the public;
- improving joint working and information sharing;
- protecting vulnerable children and improving frontline social work practice;
- stopping offenders by deploying the same range of techniques and resources as are used for other forms of organised crime;
- supporting victims and survivors.

Doubtless many of the proposed measures are necessary and will do some good. However, a study of serious case reviews investigating child sexual exploitation and child sexual abuse reveals a deep social and cultural malaise that will not and cannot be resolved by better accountability structures, improvements in reporting and information sharing procedures, enhanced inter-agency working, and investment in staff training and support for victims.

In the following section, we show how the evidence from serious case reviews published in the past five years clearly demonstrates that fundamental flaws in professional attitudes towards underage sexual activity have directly contributed to exploitation and abuse. Then, in Part Two, we shall consider some of the roots that are feeding and informing these attitudes. At this point it becomes clear that an effective strategy against child sexual exploitation demands a fundamental review of government policy on consent, underage sexual activity and the provision of contraception to young people under the age of 16.[13]

---

12 HM Government, *Tackling Child Sexual Exploitation, op. cit*, p.11.

13 The serious case reviews and independent inquiry considered in this book relate to cases in England and most of the legislation referred to relates to England and Wales, but the lessons to be drawn have wider application.

PART I
THE EVIDENCE

In the following pages, we shall examine several serious case reviews and one independent inquiry undertaken in recent years, with a particular focus on the attitudes of professionals towards sexual activity among minors. Since 2013, the NSPCC has published a chronological list of the executive summaries or full overview reports of serious case reviews, significant case reviews or multi-agency child practice reviews in England.[1]

Other parts of the UK have their own systems in place to learn from cases: in Wales they are known as child practice reviews, in Northern Ireland as case management reviews, and in Scotland as significant case reviews. For the purposes of this report, we have confined our attention to serious case reviews published in England from 2013-2016 where underage sex was a prominent feature. While not a serious case review, we have also given consideration to Professor Alexis Jay's Independent Inquiry into Child Sexual Exploitation in Rotherham 1997–2013, in view of its undoubted importance for the topic under review.

As we consider the evidence arising from these reports, we shall find common themes emerging:

- A presumption that sexual activity involving children of a similar age (or with an age gap of just a few years) is consensual and will not normally involve child sexual exploitation.
- A failure to recognise that sexual activity between young people of similar ages may still involve abuse or exploitation.
- A culture in which underage sexual activity was not challenged and hence became normalised.
- A failure on the part of professionals to raise questions about underage sex or even about the identity of the father when presented with a pregnant teenager under the age of 16.
- A culture in which the response of professionals to underage sex was

1 NSPCC, Child protection in England: Serious case reviews *https://www.nspcc.org.uk/preventing-abuse/child-protection-system/england/serious-case-reviews/* Accessed 13 February 2017.

frequently limited to the confidential provision of contraception in order to reduce the risk of pregnancy or sexually transmitted infection.

- The disparity between the age at which children may access contraception and the age at which they are legally able to give consent to sexual activity.
- Confusion over the interpretation and implementation of the Fraser guidelines[2] in relation to the routine provision of contraception to under-16s, contributing to child sexual exploitation.
- An expectation that under-16s will be sexually active meaning that access to sexual health services under the age of consent was regarded as normal and positive, and therefore failed to trigger any consideration of the possibility that the girls might be suffering abuse.
- Young people feeling let down by professionals prioritising patient confidentiality over safeguarding.
- A tendency to dismiss parental concerns and to regard parents as part of the problem.
- Children being treated as adults, with the competence and autonomy to make their own choices in relation to sexual activity.

To date, these themes have so far been largely overlooked by agencies and governmental bodies seeking to identify and implement measures aimed at protecting young people from sexual exploitation and abuse.

2 See p. 19.

A NOTE ON SERIOUS CASE REVIEWS

A serious case review is undertaken by a Local Safeguarding Children Board (LSCB) where:

(a) abuse or neglect of a child is known or suspected; and

(b) either (i) the child has died; or (ii) the child has been seriously harmed and there is cause for concern as to the way in which the authority, their Board partners or other relevant persons have worked together to safeguard the child.[1]

The final decision as to whether a serious case review is initiated rests with the chair of the LSCB. The lead reviewer should be suitably qualified and independent of the LSCB and the organisations involved in the case.

The LSCB is responsible for ensuring that there is appropriate representation in the review process of professionals and organisations who were involved with the child and family. The objective is to identify important factors in the case with a view to agreeing an action plan for necessary improvements to be made.

Where possible, the LSCB should aim to complete the serious case review within six months. The report should then be published on the LSCB website for a minimum of 12 months and made available upon request thereafter. The final report should:

- *provide a sound analysis of what happened in the case, and why, and what needs to happen in order to reduce the risk of recurrence;*
- *be written in plain English and in a way that can be easily understood by professionals and the public alike; and*
- *be suitable for publication without needing to be amended or redacted.*[2]

1 Local Safeguarding Children Boards Regulations 2006, Regulation 5.

2 HM Government, *Working Together to Safeguard Children*, op. cit, pp.78-79.

CHAPTER 1

Torbay (2013)

> *'Underage sexual activity by young people between thirteen and sixteen years old is judged on the perception that if it takes place with partners of a similar age, it is by mutual consent.'*[1]

OVERVIEW

This serious case review was concerned with the sexual abuse and exploitation of a number of girls by a small number of young men in the Torbay area between 2006 and 2011. It was instigated following the completion of Operation Mansfield, a multi-agency operation led by Devon and Cornwall Police. The operation culminated in the conviction of one male and the cautioning of another for sexual offences against several young girls.

The girls selected to be subjects of this serious case review were not all connected and were involved with one of the males at different times between 2006 and 2011:

- Two girls were looked-after children. They knew each other for a period of three weeks in 2007 when they were in the same foster placement in Torbay.
- One girl was involved with the male in 2007, but did not have links with the other girls.
- Two of the girls were friends and became involved from 2009 onwards with a number of males; again these girls were not known to the other girls.[2]

Unlike other recent high profile cases, there is no clear evidence that the abuse and exploitation perpetrated in Torbay was highly organised. The girls involved were 'abused by a small group of white males, only two of whom had any substantial evidence against them'.

---

1 Brian Boxall & Jane Wonnacott, *Serious Case Review Executive Summary, Case 26*, Torbay Safeguarding Children Board, February 2013, para 5.12. The full report has not been published.

2 *Ibid.*, para 3.2.

The executive summary of the review describes the exploitation as 'an unorganised and opportunistic abuse of vulnerable young girls for the gratification of a small group of relatively young males, linked to the supply and misuse of drugs and alcohol.'[3]

When sexual activity was identified in young girls, neither health professionals nor other professionals provided effective assessments of vulnerability or interventions.

ANALYSIS

The review noted that professionals had frequently justified or excused the girls' sexual activity and drug and alcohol abuse as 'their choice' or 'adolescent behaviour'. As a result agencies had failed to consider their behaviour as a reaction to longer-term deeper issues or current abusive relationships.[4]

The review found that professionals across different fields had failed both to recognise the abuse to which the girls were being subjected and to take necessary action:

> [W]hen sexual activity was identified in young girls, neither health professionals (when consulted for contraception and sexual health advice), nor other professionals (when such relationships were identified), provided effective assessments of vulnerability or interventions.[5]

All too often the instinctive professional response to underage sexual activity was limited to the confidential provision of contraception in order to reduce the risk of pregnancy or the spread of sexually transmitted infections (STIs). The review noted that:

> The sexual health professional focus was, understandably, on providing a confidential service with a view to preventing pregnancy or various sexual health problems. The action taken was justified by the use of Fraser Guidelines, but the assessments, which were not always recorded, failed to consider fully the girls' emotional and intellectual maturity in line with the Gillick competences. Decisions were being made on their level of understanding of the treatment proposed, that is, contraception only.[6]

3 *Ibid.*, para 5.1.
4 *Ibid.*, para 5.4.
5 *Ibid.*, para 5.8.
6 *Ibid.*, para 5.9. The term 'Gillick competence' refers to an assessment made by professionals to determine

Fraser guidelines

As in other parts of the country, health professionals in Torbay appealed to the 'Fraser guidelines' to defend the routine and confidential provision of contraception to a girl under the age of consent provided that: (i) she will understand the advice given; (ii) she cannot be persuaded to tell her parents; (iii) she is likely to begin or continue in a sexual relationship; (iv) her physical or mental health may suffer if contraceptive treatment is denied her; and (v) it is in her best interests. However, few are aware that Lord Fraser added that these criteria:

> ought not to be regarded as a licence for doctors to disregard the wishes of parents on this matter whenever they find it convenient to do so. Any doctor who behaves in such a way would, in my opinion, be failing to discharge his professional responsibilities, and I would expect him to be disciplined by his own professional body accordingly.[7]

While Lord Fraser ruled in 1985 that 'it would and should be most unusual for a doctor to advise a child without the knowledge and consent of parents on contraceptive matters', the exception swiftly become the norm. It is now frequently assumed that an underage girl is demonstrating maturity and responsibility simply by virtue of requesting contraception.

The serious case review accordingly noted that: 'There is a potential confusion regarding the way in which Fraser guidance and Gillick competencies are interpreted and implemented,' and recommended that:

> Torbay Safeguarding Children Board should bring the findings of this review to the attention of the Department of Health in respect of potential confusion regarding the Fraser guidelines and Gillick competencies.[8]

Confusion surrounding the implementation of the Fraser guidelines was by no means limited to Torbay. As the report noted:

> This review believes this is a national issue, since sexual health provision is driven by targets related to pregnancy and sexual health with the result that protection has been lost in the process.[9]

---

whether or not a child under the age of 16 may consent to medical treatment without the involvement of his or her parent. It takes its name from the House of Lords ruling against Mrs Victoria Gillick who had mounted a legal challenge against the confidential provision of contraception to under-16s.

7 Gillick v West Norfolk and Wisbech Area Health Authority and another - [1985] 3 All ER 402.

8 Boxall & Wonnacott, *Serious Case Review*, op. cit., para 7.4.

9 *Ibid.*, para 5.11.

It recognised 'a need to the review of the national guidelines in light of the growing knowledge about sexual exploitation' and recommended that:

> Torbay Safeguarding Children Board should bring the findings of this review to the attention of the Department of Health and request that steps are taken to ensure that where a young person under the age of sixteen requests contraception a full assessment is made of their social circumstances.[10]

This is a national issue, since sexual health provision is driven by targets related to pregnancy and sexual health, with the result that protection has been lost in the process.

Complacency

The report also questioned complacent attitudes towards underage sexual activity involving young people close in age, in the light of evidence suggesting that it cannot be assumed that such relationships are consensual:

> Underage sexual activity by young people between thirteen and sixteen years old is judged on the perception that if it takes place with partners of a similar age, it is by mutual consent. This perception has to be reconsidered in light of the growing evidence in this case that the abusers were not much older than the girls and also that the girls, who often did not consider that they were being abused, lied about the age of their partners as they were aware of the potential professional response. There appears to be a need to review current national guidelines to examine if they are sufficiently robust to account fully for the growing evidence around sexual activity and its links to sexual exploitation.[11]

The perception that sexual relationships involving two young teenagers are consensual is commonly held by professionals from a range of disciplines, including police officers and 'needs to be challenged', the report declared. It went on to call for a 'more considered holistic assessment' to be taken of such sexual activity, 'so that, for example, a thirteen year old who is disclosing a sexual relationship, a history of several partners and a desire to be pregnant is considered to be potentially vulnerable'.[12]

10 *Ibid.*, para 7.2.
11 *Ibid.*, para 5.12.
12 *Ibid.*, para 5.14.

CHAPTER 2
Liverpool (2013)

'Generally, Child D was seen as a child in terms of her ability to care for Child E, but otherwise as an adult making her own choices on issues such as where she lived, pregnancies and lifestyle.'[1]

OVERVIEW

Child D lived with her mother and two brothers in a caring family home. In August 2007, the mother of 14 year-old Child D took her daughter to their GP, who confirmed that Child D was pregnant. Given the stage of her pregnancy (around 19 weeks), it was evident that she had conceived at the age of 13.

The father of Child D's baby was around 18 months older than Child D and lived with his family in the same area. He was a persistent offender who used and dealt in Class A drugs and abused alcohol. At times he made life unpleasant for Child D and her family. Although he is named in the report as 'Adult 1', he was, in fact, a child until late December 2009.

Child D initially planned to have an abortion, but subsequently changed her mind and a referral was made to the midwifery department. The baby (Child E) was born in February 2008. The father was present at the birth, but his details were not requested by the hospital staff.

Towards the end of the same month, Adult 1 (then aged 16) violently assaulted Child D, inflicting facial and other injuries on her which were treated in hospital. He was charged with assault occasioning actual bodily harm. He was placed on police bail, but remanded in custody after breaching the bail conditions. In April 2008, however, the charges were dropped after Child D decided that she no longer wished to pursue the matter. But from late December 2008 until April 2010, Adult 1 was in prison for several crimes, including drug and dishonesty offences.

1 Liverpool Safeguarding Children Board, *Overview report: Serious case review incorporating a domestic homicide review: child D*, February 2012, para 1.2.33. The report is dated February 2012, but was not published until 10 May 2013.

The GP confirming the pregnancy did not think to raise the question of underage sex or the identity of the father.

In early 2009, Child D (now aged 15) began a relationship with Adult 2. He was five years older than her with a significant criminal history. He had assaulted a previous partner and dominated Child D's life to such an extent that he held her prisoner for over two weeks in his house and ensured that she did not see Child E. In mid-August, he inflicted burns on Child D's face with a hot iron. He was arrested, convicted of assault and sentenced to 42 months imprisonment from November 2009.

In April 2010 Adult 1 was released and resumed an on-and-off relationship with Child D, marked by violence at times. A year later, in April 2011, Child D died and Adult 1 was subsequently convicted of murder and sentenced to life imprisonment.

ANALYSIS

Although Child D was only 13 when she became pregnant, the evidence of her underage sexual activity was viewed with complacency by all the agencies with whom she was in contact and did not trigger any further enquiries or action.

The overview report of the Serious Case Review records that:

> The GP confirming the pregnancy did not think to raise the question of underage sex or the identity of the father with Child D, Mother, practice colleagues or children's services. This is an oversight for which no explanation is offered.[2]

The report adds that: 'The Overview Panel felt that agencies missed a significant opportunity to complete a thorough assessment of the family's needs; including the issue of underage sex.'[3]

Missed opportunities

In a particularly damning section, the overview report states:

> Child E was born in February 2008. A simple calculation shows that Child D was sexually active at 13 years of age meaning she had engaged in an unlawful act, which probably continued until she reached 16 years of age as evidenced

2 *Ibid.*, para 3.3.3.
3 *Ibid.*, para 3.3.8.

by her contraception requirements. No agency addressed the unlawful aspect of Child D's sexual activity. Child D gave no indication that she was an unwilling party to sexual activity; albeit there is no evidence that anyone explored that point with her. From a health perspective the screening procedures to determine if Child D was at risk of significant harm through her sexual activity were not undertaken. There were many opportunities in Child D's engagement with agencies where the impact of her being sexually active should have been explored.[4]

There were many opportunities in Child D's engagement with agencies where the impact of her being sexually active should have been explored.

The issue of the age of consent in relation to Child D featured in the terms of reference for the serious case review. The question was raised:

> What significance did agencies attach to the age gap between Child D and her partners, Adult 1 and Adult 2 particularly with regard to Child D and the age of sexual consent? [5]

In addressing this question, the review panel noted that Adult 1 was 18 months older than Child D and that Adult 2 was four years and 10 months older than her. With regard to the relationship with Adult 1, the overview report records that Child D was 'engaged in unlawful sexual activity for about three years'. It also notes that 'several agencies knew of Child D's pregnancy and eventually all did', though 'not all knew Adult 1's age because they failed to ask Child D'.

While 'the general view was that the 18 month gap was not significant', the overview panel concluded that 'more significance should have been given by assessing agencies to emotional age, rather than actual age'.[6]

Unlawful sexual activity

Child D began her relationship with Adult 2 a few months before her 16th birthday in July 2009. It is therefore 'likely that he was having unlawful sexual relations with her'. Although there are increased sentencing powers where someone over the age of 18 engages in unlawful sexual

4 *Ibid.*, para 5.3.3.
5 *Ibid.*, para 2.3.2.
6 *Ibid.*, paras 5.6.1-2.

activity with someone under the age of 16, in this instance the agencies failed to recognise 'the potential power imbalance'. The overview report observes that:

> In April 2009 [a professional] noted that Child D was not living at home but did not follow it up. Child D was a few months short of her 16th birthday and it is likely she was living with Adult 2 and engaged in under age *(sic)* sex. The police and children's services knew in July 2009, just after Child D turned 16 years that she and Adult 2 were in a relationship, but there is no evidence that any thought was given to the age gap. .. His greater age and Child D's level of maturity made her more susceptible to sexual exploitation.[7]

Arising from this case, Children's Services Liverpool made the following recommendation, among others:

> Where a child of 13 years or younger becomes pregnant, midwifery services and/or the family GP should always refer the matter to Children's Services. In each case, Children's Services should undertake the Initial Assessment, should liaise with all relevant agencies including the police and should make enquiries regarding the identity of, and any information known about, the father of the unborn child.[8]

7 *Ibid.*, para 5.6.3.

8 *Ibid.*, para 9.2.3.

CHAPTER 3
Rochdale (2013)

'The drive to reduce teenage pregnancy, whilst commendable in itself, is believed to have contributed to a culture whereby professionals may have become inured to early sexual activity in young teenagers.'[1]

OVERVIEW

Rochdale Borough Safeguarding Children Board published overview reports of two serious case reviews in December 2013.

The first report relates to six young people (YP1-6) who were subjected to serious and prolonged child sexual exploitation during their teenage years by a group of Asian men who they met in takeaways and through contact with taxi firms. All six had considerable involvement with a wide range of services in Rochdale including Children's Social Care (CSC), health services, the police and voluntary organisations. They came from three different families and did not all know each other, though there were some links between them.[2]

The second report concerns one young person (YP7), who experienced serious and repeated sexual exploitation as a child. She, too, was involved with a wide range of services. This second review ran parallel with the larger review.[3]

The purpose of the two serious case reviews was to identify whether agencies which provided services to these young people, acted appropriately and to establish what needs to be learned from their experience, with a view to reviewing practice.

ANALYSIS

The serious case review of the six young women concluded that a preoccupation with reducing teenage pregnancy rates had encouraged a

---

1 Rochdale Borough Safeguarding Children Board, *The Overview Report of the Serious Case Review in respect of Young People 1,2,3,4,5 & 6*, December 2013, [Hereafter *Rochdale 1-6*], para 4.3.46.

2 *Ibid.*, para 3.1.

3 Rochdale Borough Safeguarding Children Board, *The Overview Report of the Serious Case Review in respect of Young Person 7*, [Hereafter *Rochdale 7*] December 2013.

culture in which underage sexual activity went unchallenged and many young people were placed at risk of sexual exploitation.

Agencies such as Children's Social Care, health services and the police failed to protect them because they 'simply assumed that the young people were making a "lifestyle choice"'.[4] In the words of the father of one of the girls, 'It's what they expected of our children',[5] and so the fact that the teenagers frequently accessed health services in relation to sexual activity, sexually transmitted infections and pregnancy, failed to trigger any consideration that they might be suffering abuse.

Damage limitation

The report suggests that professionals in Rochdale had become complacent about underage sexual activity and had been so focussed on a damage limitation exercise aimed at reducing teenage conception and sexually transmitted infection rates that they had failed to act in the best interests of vulnerable young people. The report states:

> The drive to reduce teenage pregnancy, whilst commendable in itself, is believed to have contributed to a culture whereby professionals may have become inured to early sexual activity in young teenagers. The culture from the top of organisations concerned with teenage pregnancy focused on meeting targets for the reduction of teenage conception and sexually transmitted diseases sometimes to the detriment of an alternative focus - the possibility that a young person has been or is at risk of harm and action other than clinical responses are required.[6]

The mother of some of the girls repeatedly raised concerns with the police about the safety of her daughters and the men they were spending time with, and the teenagers themselves made allegations. Yet the allegations were either not properly referred to the lead statutory agencies or else investigations were not effectively concluded.

Even when two of the teenagers requested an abortion there is no evidence that professionals enquired further into the nature of the sexual relationships they were engaged in. One of the girls, aged 14, asked the school nurse for a pregnancy test. When the test proved positive, she was referred to the crisis intervention team (CIT), an NHS body offering confidential specialist sexual health advice for young people, including

---

4 *Rochdale 1-6*, op. cit., para 4.3.21.

5 *Ibid.*, para 4.7.15.

6 *Ibid.*, para 4.3.46.

those aged under 16. The report relates:

> There is no evidence that consideration was given to safeguarding concerns despite her age, the stated age of the father and her known home circumstances.

> [The girl] told CIT that she had had sex two weeks previously with a 21 year old man, that she had not seen him since and that she did not want her mother to know. The option of termination was discussed with her, but there is no evidence that the fact that this 14 year old girl had had sex with a man considerably older than her was pursued any further.
>
> [She] subsequently attended at the hospital for a termination. It is of concern that the focus appears to have been purely on the clinical need. There is no evidence that consideration was given to safeguarding concerns despite [her] age, the stated age of the father and her known home circumstances.[7]

Fundamental misconceptions

The report observes that repeated failings over a period of five years in relation to six young people who were in contact with at least 17 different agencies cannot be accounted for by negligence on the part of front-line workers. There were, rather, 'fundamental problems and obstacles at a strategic level' and it was 'absolutely clear that the problems were much more deep rooted than can be explained as failings at an individual level'.[8]

The report refers to 'widely held and deep rooted attitudes' on the part of professionals whose assumption that the teenagers were making meaningful choices about how they lived their lives was 'fundamentally misconceived'.[9] It also notes that the six instances of child sexual exploitation it covers were not isolated cases:

> [T]he experiences of these 6 young people whilst fundamentally important in their own right are accepted by agencies within Rochdale as being indicative of the experience of other young people at the time.[10]

A separate report documented the failure of child protection agencies in Rochdale to protect a seventh child, even though they were aware

7 *Ibid.*, para 4.3.29-30.
8 *Ibid.*, para 4.9.6.
9 *Ibid.*, paras 4.7.14-15.
10 *Ibid.*, para 4.9.6.

that she had had a number of sexual partners at the age of 13. She informed staff at the sexual health clinic that she had been forced to engage in sexual activity against her wishes and that the men had hit her if she refused, and yet no report was made to the police or Children's Social Care. As with the six teenage girls covered in the other report, agencies felt that they were not in a position to take action to protect 'Young Person 7' due to 'the perception that she placed herself in these settings by choice'. The report records:

Staff have to some degree become desensitised to what risks are viewed as 'normal'.

> One of the agencies, Rochdale Borough Housing has identified that staff…have to some degree become desensitised to what risks are viewed as 'normal', seeing them as something that their client group may not be able to avoid. This once again linked with a tendency to refer to YP7's lifestyle, or making choices, which is a fundamental misunderstanding of the response of victims of sexual exploitation.[11]

Unintended consequences

The revelation in the two Rochdale reports that professionals working for agencies charged with the care and protection of young people may be inadvertently aiding and abetting child abusers should prompt an urgent review of professional attitudes towards underage sexual activity. In Rochdale and elsewhere, giving young people free access to 'sexual health services' on the assumption that 'they are going to have sex anyway, so we must do what we can to reduce the risk' has proved to be anything but compassionate. Serious questions need to be raised about the unintended consequences of the confidential provision of contraception, abortion and treatment for sexually transmitted infections.

The two overview reports concerning the sexual exploitation of seven teenage girls in Rochdale repeatedly assert that less than a decade ago child protection professionals failed to recognise child sexual exploitation. For example, the reports state:

- The exploitation of children for the sexual gratification of adults is far from a new phenomenon, but what is comparatively new is a shift in societal understanding

11 *Rochdale 7*, op. cit., para 4.4.17.

of this phenomenon. As recently as 5 years ago, the sexual exploitation of children was largely defined as child prostitution, by implication a disturbing social evil rather than something that was recognised unequivocally as child abuse.[12]

- What has become evident in relation to all these young people, is that despite considerable information being available to many of the agencies that they were extremely vulnerable and that there was evidence they were involved sexually with older men, the possibility that they were experiencing sexual exploitation was not recognised by the key statutory agencies until the middle of 2008.[13]
- With hindsight we can now identify a number of indicators that YP7 may have been experiencing child sexual exploitation from the outset, including: symptoms of sexually transmitted infections and YP7's statement that she had had a number of sexual partners at the age of 13. These could not necessarily have been expected to lead to consideration of CSE at the time given the level of awareness across agencies in 2004.[14]

12 *Rochdale 1-6*, op. cit., para 4.2.2.
13 *Ibid.*, para 4.3.2.
14 *Rochdale 7*, op. cit., para 4.4.1.

CHAPTER 4
Rotherham (2014)

'Children as young as 11 were deemed to be having consensual sexual intercourse when in fact they were being raped and abused by adults'[1]

OVERVIEW

> No one knows the true scale of sexual exploitation in Rotherham over the years. Our conservative estimate is that there were more than 1,400 victims in the period covered by the Inquiry, and an unknown number who were at risk of being exploited.[2]

So begins Alexis Jay's Independent Inquiry into Child Sexual Exploitation in Rotherham between 1997–2013. The facts are as stark as they are harrowing. Children, including girls as young as 11 were:

- raped by multiple perpetrators,
- trafficked to other towns and cities in the north of England,
- abducted, beaten, and intimidated,
- in some cases, doused in petrol and threatened with being set alight,
- threatened with guns,
- made to witness brutally violent rapes, and threatened that they would be next if they told anyone.

In just over a third of cases, children affected by sexual exploitation were previously known to services 'because of child protection and neglect'. Within social care, the scale and seriousness of the problem was underplayed by senior managers. No less than three reports setting out the situation in Rotherham (published in 2002, 2003 and 2006) were either suppressed or ignored. And there was evidence in many files that prior to 2007, child victims from around the age of eleven upwards were not viewed as a priority for children's social care, even when they were being sexually abused and exploited.

1 Alexis Jay OBE, *Independent Inquiry into Child Sexual Exploitation in Rotherham 1997–2013*, August 2014, para 8.1.

2 Ibid., p.1.

According to the report, 'This abuse is not confined to the past but continues to this day.'[3]

ANALYSIS

The authorities in Rotherham displayed the same complacency towards underage sex that had characterised agencies in Rochdale who failed to protect vulnerable girls because they 'assumed that the young people were making a 'lifestyle choice'. The Rotherham Inquiry found that 'children as young as 11 were deemed to be having consensual sexual intercourse when in fact they were being raped and abused by adults'.[4] For example, the report relates that:

> Several social work practitioners told us that they were aware of the problem of the sexual exploitation of children in Rotherham from the early to mid-1990s, although it was not well recognised or understood and was often described as 'child prostitution'.[5]

Blaming children and their parents

'Child D' may be taken as a specific example of the consequences for a vulnerable young person when the authorities effectively hold her responsible for the abuse she suffers:

> Child D (2003) was 13 when she was groomed by a violent sexual predator who raped and trafficked her. Her parents, Risky Business [Rotherham's youth project] and Child D herself all understood the seriousness of the abuse, violence and intimidation she suffered. Police and children's social care were ineffective and seemed to blame the child. A core assessment was done but could not be traced on the file. An initial assessment accurately described the risks to Child D but appeared to blame her for 'placing herself at risk of sexual exploitation and danger'.[6]

In some instances, the parents of the young people were at least to some extent aware of what was happening to their daughters, but their concerns were dismissed by the authorities. The report records that:

---

3 *Ibid.*

4 *Ibid.*, para 8.1.

5 *Ibid.*, para 5.20.

6 *Ibid.*, para 5.24.

> In two of the cases..., fathers tracked down their daughters and tried to remove them from houses where they were being abused, only to be arrested themselves when police were called to the scene. In a small number of cases...the victims were arrested for offences such as breach of the peace or being drunk and disorderly, with no action taken against the perpetrators of rape and sexual assault against children.[7]

The social worker's assessment was that Child C's mother was not able to accept her growing up.

Or, to take another example:

> Child C (2002) was 14 when sexual exploitation was identified... Her mother voiced her concerns about Child C being sexually active, going missing and repeated incidents of severe intoxication when she had been plied with drink by older males. Several initial assessments were carried out and some family support was offered. The case was then closed. The social worker's assessment was that Child C's mother was not able to accept her growing up. In fact, she was displaying what are now known to be classic indicators of child sexual exploitation from the age of 11. By the age of 13, she was at risk from violent perpetrators, associating with other victims of sexual exploitation, misusing drugs, and at high risk.[8]

Ignoring the law

The inquiry was told that: '[T]he attitude of the Police at that time seemed to be that [the young women] were all 'undesirables' and...not worthy of police protection.'[9] But as Kay Kelly of the Barnardo's Turnaround Service in Bradford has noted, ignoring the law on the age of consent blinds child protection agencies to the enormity of the abuse that is being perpetrated and exposes children to the risk of sexual exploitation:

> The reality wasn't recognised. These young people weren't seen as victims. They were very much seen as perpetrators themselves and treated as adult prostitutes. Of course they weren't, because they were all under the legal age for consent.[10]

7 *Ibid.*, para 5.9.
8 *Ibid.*, para 5.23.
9 *Ibid.*, para 8.2.
10 *Ibid.*, Appendix 4, p.132.

Amid fears that Rotherham is far from an isolated case and that similar cases of abuse are occurring in towns and cities across the country, local authorities were instructed to take note of Professor Jay's report. In a joint letter, the then Education Secretary Nicky Morgan and Communities Secretary Eric Pickles, urged council leaders to consider whether they had adequate measures in place to ensure that they could not be accused of similar failings.[11]

Much of the media coverage of the Rotherham report focussed on the failure of the authorities to act for fear of being accused of racism. The Labour MP for Rochdale, Simon Danczuk, described a culture where 'political correctness and cultural sensitivity are more important than child rape', where 'managers become more interested in ticking boxes in diversity training than protecting children', and where 'social-work bosses ban families from looking after children because they're members of Ukip and not sufficiently versed in multiculturalism'.[12]

However, as the evidence cited above demonstrates, the inquiry also serves to illustrate the damaging consequences of viewing sexual activity among minors as a normal part of growing up.

11 Rt Hon Nicky Morgan and Rt Hon Eric Pickles, letter to Leader of Principal Councils in England on 'Safeguarding vulnerable children', 24 September 2014.

12 Simon Danczuk, 'Rotherham is not an isolated incident', *Daily Telegraph*, 31 August 2014.

CHAPTER 5
Thurrock (2014)

'Finding 1: There is a pattern whereby national and local policy agendas have driven practice in relation to underage sexual activity to have a stronger focus on sexual health and teenage pregnancy rather than sexual abuse/exploitation.'[1]

OVERVIEW

This serious case review relates to a girl named in the report as Julia, who had a long history of contact with children's welfare and child protection services.

In total, Julia made four disclosures of rape by boys aged 15-18 over a three year period when she was aged between 12-15. Despite police investigations, it had not been possible to achieve a prosecution.[2]

In November 2010, when Julia was aged 12, she told someone at her school that she had been sexually assaulted by a boy who was a friend. The school alerted Children's Social Care, who tried to make contact with Julia's mother without success, and also contacted the police, who visited the family home that evening. At the school's suggestion, Julia's mother took her to see the GP. The GP prescribed contraception and agreed to contact the police, though there is no recorded evidence that this happened.

In January 2011, the police said that the rape disclosure was not supported by the available evidence, so no further action could be taken.

During June and July 2011, Julia's mother sought support from social services in relation to Julia's disruptive behaviour and sexual contact with boys. A social worker made a referral to parenting support and the sexual health advisor.

---

1 Jane Wiffen and David Peplow, *Serious Case Review: 'Julia'*, Thurrock Local Safeguarding Children Board, December 2014, p.32.

2 The report is not explicit on this point, but suggests that the difficulties in achieving a prosecution may have been in connection with Julia's learning difficulties and her difficult early childhood experiences making it less than straightforward for her to provide a clear picture of what had actually taken place. *Ibid.*, see para 2.25.

The following month, Children's Social Care closed the case, only to re-open the file in September 2011 when Julia's mother told hospital staff that Julia had been sexually active since the age of 11.

Contraception

In November 2011, Julia attended a sexual health drop-in session with the school nurse. She said that she was having sexual contact with a 14 year-old boy and that her mother was aware. She was assessed as Gillick competent and contraceptive advice and support was given, in line with existing health guidance.

In May 2012, Julia and her mother consulted a GP twice regarding the contraceptive pill and once for advice regarding the mother's concerns about Julia's behaviour. Later that summer, in June and August, Julia's mother contacted the Duty Social Work Team twice to seek advice about managing Julia's behaviour in general, her sexual behaviour in particular, and her desire to meet boys.

During the course of an investigation of the sexual assault of another young woman in October 2012, the police were told that Julia had also been raped by the same perpetrator. The police interviewed Julia and she alleged that she too had been raped. However, in a subsequent police interview, she said that it had been consensual and that she had previously had sex with six other boys. The police made a referral to Children's Social Care and a core assessment was initiated.

However, this assessment was not completed before Julia, now aged 14, reported to the police in December 2012 that she had been raped by a 19 year-old man. She was seen at the Sexual Assault Referral Centre where she was diagnosed with a sexually transmitted infection. The nurse made a referral to Children's Social Care because she was concerned about the attitude of both Julia and her mother towards the infection.

A few days later, Julia and her mother attended the Genito-Urinary Medicine Department of Sexual Health for treatment. Julia's mother told the doctor that her daughter had had '15 to 20 sexual partners'. The nurse at the clinic made a further referral to Children's Social Care.

As a result of Julia's disclosure of rape in December 2012, she was made the subject of a child protection plan in February 2013.

The focus was on sexual health advice rather than safeguarding.

The designated nurse at the Sexual Assault Referral Centre referred the details of Julia's history to the Thurrock Serious Case Review sub-committee. In their judgment, the case met the criteria for undertaking a serious case review

ANALYSIS

The serious case review notes:

> The sexual assault and rape of a 12 year old child is a serious issue… The law makes clear that children under 13 are particularly vulnerable, so to protect younger children any sexual activity with a child aged 12 or under will be subject to the maximum penalties – whatever the age of the perpetrator.[3]

Yet, when Julia's mother disclosed that Julia had been raped six weeks before her 13th birthday, the GP prescribed contraception. The report observes that:

> [T]here is no evidence that [Julia] was assessed to see whether her experiences had been abusive in line with existing policies and procedures and there was no referral to Children's Social Care. The focus was on sexual health advice rather than safeguarding.[4]

The priority given to sexual health over child protection is reflected in the first finding of the review:

> There is a pattern whereby national and local policy agendas have driven practice in relation to underage sexual activity to have a stronger focus on sexual health and teenage pregnancy rather than sexual abuse/exploitation.[5]

Government priorities

The report notes that 'professionals are…required to give young people advice and support about sexual relationships, contraception and sexual and

3 *Ibid.*, paras 2.23, 3.6.
4 *Ibid.*, para 3.14.
5 *Ibid.*, pp.30, 32, 65.

reproductive health including pregnancy and abortion'.[6] It further observes that successive governments have prioritised reducing teenage pregnancies and promoting sexual health.[7] Yet it highlights a possible conflict between meeting sexual health targets and protecting children and young people:

There was a contradiction in policy which makes underage sexual relationships illegal, whilst at the same time recognising the need for support when it takes place in the context of choice and consent.

> Although this policy guidance now makes clear that all professionals providing sexual health advice must be aware of child protection and safeguarding issues as well as having guidelines and referral pathways in place for risk assessment and management of child sexual abuse, there remains a potential contradiction between the responsibility to address sexual exploitation and promote positive sexual health.[8]

The report goes on to refer to 'an underlying tension inherent within the different role that professionals play',[9] but with a consistent focus on sexual health advice at the expense of child protection. Julia made allegations of sexual assault and sought sexual health advice on numerous occasions, and yet 'on each occasion there was a stronger professional focus on advice-giving rather than exploring issues of consent and abuse'.[10]

Thus, when Julia sought contraceptive advice at the school sexual health drop-in session, the school nurse provided her with contraception on the basis that she demonstrated sufficient maturity without considering the broader issues. The review therefore speaks of a 'contradiction in policy which makes underage sexual relationships illegal, whilst at the same time recognising the need for support when it takes place in the context of choice and consent'.[11]

In the judgment of the authors of the Thurrock serious case review, part of an effective response to the increased awareness and heightened state of alert regarding child sexual exploitation, 'will be to ensure that there

6 *Ibid.*, para 3.11.
7 *Ibid.*, para 3.12.
8 *Ibid.*, para 3.13.
9 *Ibid.*, para 3.17.
10 *Ibid.*
11 *Ibid.*, para 3.19.

is a professional balance between appropriate advice regarding sexual health and a heightened awareness that this might be an opportunity to consider the potential for sexual exploitation'.[12]

The importance of the GP's role in identifying sexual exploitation and abuse is underlined:

> GPs are a critical part of the safeguarding network. It is essential that any barriers to their effective engagement in safeguarding processes are actively addressed. This is particularly important in the context of underage sexual activity and sexual exploitation, where GPs are likely to be a key point of contact for young people.[13]

Child-centred record-keeping

The review also highlights some of the risks associated with a child-centred approach to maintaining records. The report records that:

> The Review Team and Case Group told us that it was common practice across all agencies to record what children and young people told them uncritically, in the context of early sexual experiences. They considered that professionals understood the importance of recording what young people told them as a way of being child centred.[14]

Specific reference is made to the terms 'allegations' of rape, 'consent' to sexual activity, multiple 'partners' and 'risky behaviour'. Such language was recorded in professional records 'without any clear critique or analysis about what it meant for Julia and her well-being'.[15] For example, 'Julia needed professionals to help her see what had happened to her was not actually consensual',[16] and the use of the word 'partner' had 'the potential to make her experiences of sexual exploitation hidden'.[17]

The review emphasises that, 'This language needed to be challenged, and addressed, not recorded without comment.'[18]

In its second finding, the review accordingly concludes that:

> If professionals record the language used by young people and their parents

12 *Ibid.*, p.36.
13 *Ibid.*, p. 59.
14 *Ibid.*, para 3.26.
15 *Ibid.*, para 2.23.
16 *Ibid.*, para 3.23.
17 *Ibid.*, para 3.24.
18 *Ibid.*, para 2.23.

regarding early sexually exploitative experiences without clear analysis and challenge it has the potential to leave children and young people without an adequate response or protection.[19]

19 *Ibid.*, para 3.19.

CHAPTER 6
Oxfordshire (2015)

'The law around consent was not properly understood, and the Review finds confusion related to a national culture where children are sexualised at an ever younger age and deemed able to consent to, say, contraception long before they are able legally to have sex. A professional tolerance to knowing young teenagers were having sex with adults seems to have developed.'[1]

OVERVIEW

The serious case review into child sexual exploitation in Oxfordshire focused on the experiences of six girls aged between 12-16 who were the victims of offences committed between May 2004 and June 2012. These six girls constituted a small fraction of approximately 370 girls and young women who had been identified as possible victims of sexual exploitation in Oxfordshire within the previous 16 years.

In the words of the Oxfordshire Safeguarding Children Board (OSCB):

> The children were groomed by their abusers and were given alcohol and drugs, gifts and attention, and led to believe that the men were their boyfriends. They were forced to have sex and were physically assaulted, threatened, drugged, raped, trafficked and sold for sex. They were pulled into a frightening world where they felt unable to escape. Some parents and carers raised concerns. Sometimes their concerns were not given the weight they deserved and sometimes no action was taken by professionals.[2]

'Operation Bullfinch', a complex investigation led by the police and involving OSCB partners identified a significant number of children as victims of serious sexual exploitation. Nine men stood trial at the Old

1 Alan Bedford, *Serious Case Review into Child Sexual Exploitation in Oxfordshire: from the experiences of Children A, B, C, D, E, and F*, approved by the Oxfordshire Safeguarding Children Board, 26 February 2015, para 1.3.

2 Oxfordshire Safeguarding Children Board, *Serious Case Review into Child Sexual Exploitation in Oxfordshire from the experiences of the children involved*, (Summary document), 2015, p.1.

Bailey in January 2013, of whom seven were convicted and received substantial custodial sentences. The charges related to six individual girls – four cases of historic abuse and two which were more recent. The abuse was described by the trial judge as a 'series of sexual crimes of the utmost depravity'.[3]

Five of the seven convicted offenders were of Pakistani heritage. No evidence was found of any agency failing to act due to racial sensitivities. The victims were all white British girls.

ANALYSIS

In her statement to the press, Maggie Blyth, the Independent Chair of the Oxfordshire Safeguarding Children Board, highlighted the key findings of the report, which included the following explanations for the systemic failings in Oxfordshire:

- The behaviour of the girls was interpreted through eyes, and a language, which saw them as young adults rather than children, and therefore assumed they had control of their actions…
- What happened to the girls was not recognised as being as terrible as it was because of a view that saw them as consenting, or bringing problems upon themselves…
- There were misguided interpretations of the law around consent, and an apparent tolerance of (or failure to be alarmed by) unlawful sexual activity
- There was insufficient understanding of parental reaction to their children's behaviour and going missing, so distraught, desperate and terrified parents were sometimes seen as part of the problem
- There was an absence of curiosity about what was happening to the girls, or to investigate further incidents or concerns.[4]

Easy access to contraception

The OSCB's brief summary of the serious case review suggests that the ease with which young people under the age of consent can access contraception is helping to facilitate abuse and exploitation. It observes that:

3 Bedford, *Serious Case Review*, op. cit., para 1.11.
4 Maggie Blyth, Independent Chair, Statement to Press Conference, March 2015.

There was confusion around the fact that young teenagers can consent to use contraception to have sex that might be illegal. This makes it easier for the exploiters. Young teenagers were seen too much as young adults rather than as children. Some professionals seemed to get used to knowing the girls were having sex with men, rather than having a clear view that it was wrong, full stop.[5]

There was confusion around the fact that young teenagers can consent to use contraception to have sex that might be illegal. This makes it easier for the exploiters.

The full report accordingly recommends that:

Relevant government departments should consider the impact of current guidance on consent to ensure what seems to be the ever-lower age at which a child can be deemed to consent (for example to treatment) and attitudes to underage sex are not making it easier for perpetrators to succeed.[6]

The serious case review notes that a passive acceptance of unlawful sexual activity was combined with a dismissive attitude towards the girls' parents, who were often kept in the dark. Parental comments included:

- 'No one thought about us – what it would be like if it was their daughter.'
- 'Police wouldn't tell us addresses so we could go and bring her home.'
- 'She was a minor but we were told it wasn't our business.'
- 'I tried to tell social services about the evidence – but they weren't interested. It was obvious it was something sexual.'
- 'I keep emphasising "she is a minor." Why would other vulnerable groups be protected from themselves, but she was allowed to make the wrong choices?'
- 'The police said she didn't appear in danger, they said she was happy to be there, and refused to tell me where she was.'[7]

The review records that 'distraught, desperate and terrified parents were sometimes seen as part of the problem'.[8] One social worker is

5 Oxfordshire Safeguarding Children Board, Brief Summary of the Serious Case Review, March 2015.
6 Bedford, *Serious Case Review*, op. cit., para 9.14.
7 *Ibid.*, para 3.14.
8 *Ibid.*, para 8.5.

reported as describing a father being 'obsessed with finding [his daughter] when she goes missing', prompting the author of the report to remark that he would be 'worried if any parent was not obsessed with finding a 13-year-old girl who has been subject to rapes, excessive drug taking and alcohol, or who was running from Council Care'.[9]

Passive acceptance

In addition to the casual attitude towards underage sex and the exclusion of parents, the third ingredient in the cocktail which left the child protection agencies paralysed was a fatal spirit of non-judgmentalism which regards young people as autonomous agents who must be left entirely free to make their own choices. In response to the cry, 'Why wasn't something done?' the report's author, Alan Bedford, concludes that:

> [T]here was...an acceptance of a degree of underage sexual activity that reflects a wider societal reluctance to consider something 'wrong'. This involves ascribing to young teenagers a degree of self-determining choice which should be respected. This is not altogether surprising when the national guidance [on health] involves an assessment of the child's ability to give true consent to receiving contraceptive advice or treatment without the involvement of parents. In a nutshell, a child may be judged mature enough to get contraceptives to have sex with an adult at an age when they are deemed in law unable to give consent to the sex itself. It is no wonder there was confusion and a lack of confidence in taking action.[10]

The report refers to 'a lack of professional curiosity' across agencies. There was, for example, 'no exploration of why a girl in a deeply troubled family was using contraceptives at 12' and no further investigation when a girl told a hospital doctor that she 'regularly [had] sex for alcohol and drugs' and described those she had intercourse with as 'friends'.[11]

There were times, we are told, when 'confidentiality was put before protection',[12] with the result that 'inappropriate or illegal sexual activity by children who were clients, patients or looked-after children was subject to a higher tolerance threshold than would be the case [with], say, the

9 *Ibid.*, para 5.113.
10 *Ibid.*, para 5.23.
11 *Ibid.*, para 5.62-3.
12 *Ibid.*, para 8.52.

average parent':

> This may have been because professionals could not find a way to stop the girls going where they were at risk; it may have been from trying to avoid being too 'controlling' and risking more alienation, and from the wide sense that 'nothing could be done'. However, for some, it may also relate to a reluctance to take a moral stance on right and wrong, and seeing being non-judgmental as the overriding principle.[13]

The review continues:

> The law regards underage sex between peers over 13 as not something that should have any intervention, and it is not much more of a step to see sex between say a 14-year-old and a young adult as 'one of those things'. And, in this Review, sex with older adults did not always lead to what might colloquially be called bringing in the cavalry to intervene come what may. The benign word 'boyfriend' disguised age-inappropriate relationships.[14]

The need for moral judgments

The review concluded that professionals must intervene decisively to protect children even if by so doing they are deemed to be acting 'judgmentally':

> In the tension between action to be non-judgmental and action to prevent harm because an activity is wrong or inappropriate, the latter should be the overriding principle with children.[15]

Other learning points included:

- Staff at all levels need to be clear about the law of consent (to sex and healthcare).
- Verbal consent does not mean it is free consent, or sensible consent.
- Across agencies, supervisors should test out with staff making decisions about how they see the threshold for action with sexually active children.
- Supervisors (and their managers) need to be aware of the tendency for the impact of an incidence of abuse or risk to lessen when such incidents happen frequently…

13 *Ibid.*, para 8.53
14 *Ibid.*
15 *Ibid.*, para 8.58, and Appendix 1, p.iii.

- Agencies which act as parent or share parental care should, when determining what is appropriate action in the face of risky behaviour, consider what a good parent caring for a child at home would do.
- There needs to be a rethink of the national guidance regarding sexually active children, to ensure that well-intentioned policies to support the vulnerable young do not inadvertently add to a climate that facilitates exploitation.[16]

There needs to be a rethink of the national guidance regarding sexually active children, to ensure that well-intentioned policies to support the vulnerable young do not inadvertently add to a climate that facilitates exploitation.

In a section on tolerance, the review calls for a national debate on some of the social and cultural and moral factors which are making it easier for abusers to exploit children and inhibiting professionals from taking necessary preventative action:

> There can be little doubt that the earlier sexualisation of children, the age of perceived self-determination and ability to consent creeping lower, and the reluctance in many places, both political and professional, to have any firm statements about something being 'wrong', creates an environment where it is easier for vulnerable young people/children to be exploited. It also makes it harder for professionals to have the confidence and bravery to be more proactive on prevention and intervention. This is an issue reaching way beyond Oxfordshire and requires a national debate.[17]

16 *Ibid.*
17 *Ibid.*, para 8.55.

CHAPTER 7
Hampshire (2015)

'Staff were made aware of the sexual activity by [Child F's] GP but judged it to be consensual and a confidential medical matter. The girl later told her parents and further information came to light that suggested the sexual activity had been non-consensual.'[1]

OVERVIEW

Stanbridge Earls School was a co-educational day and boarding school catering for pupils aged between 10-20. It specialised in teaching pupils with specific learning difficulties and special educational needs or disabilities. The school closed in September 2013 after a Special Educational Needs and Disability First Tier Tribunal (SENDIST) had expressed serious concerns earlier in the year. The adverse publicity which followed this judgment led to a decline in the number of pupils attending the school, with the result that it was no longer financially viable.

The tribunal had considered issues of disability discrimination in relation to Child F, a former female pupil of the school, and found that the school had discriminated against her in contravention of the Equality Act 2011. It specifically stated that the school had not taken all reasonable steps to keep her safe. The judgment was sent to the Secretary of State to reconsider the continuing registration of the school.

Following the closure of the school, a serious case review was conducted to investigate the safeguarding implications of the events leading up to the final outcome.[2]

ANALYSIS

Child F started attending Stanbridge Earls School in June 2010 when she was 14 years old. Soon after her admission to the school it became evident

---

1 From the NSPCC's summary of the background to the case, October 2015 – Hampshire – Child F (Stanbridge Earls School) *https://www.nspcc.org.uk/preventing-abuse/child-protection-system/case-reviews/2015/* Accessed 14 February 2017.

2 Kevin Harrington and Jane Whyte, *The safeguarding implications of events leading to the closure of Stanbridge Earls School: a serious case review*, Hampshire Safeguarding Children Board, October 2015.

that her level of social and emotional development was significantly below what might have been expected in a child of her age.

During the first six months of 2011, there were indications that Child F and others might be engaging in sexual activity at the school. The school sought to address the immediate presenting issues in an unplanned way without adequate recognition that there might be underlying issues to be considered, including concern for Child F's welfare.

Staff took a view that this sexual activity was both 'consensual' and a confidential medical matter.

Assumptions

Towards the end of June 2011 Child F received medical treatment from the school's GP and evidence emerged that she had been involved in sexual activity. The report states that:

> Staff took a view that this sexual activity was both 'consensual' and a confidential medical matter. They acceded to a request from Child F, aged 15, that her parents should not be informed. The matter was not reported to other members of staff, the CSD [Children's Services Department], the police, or to the parents of the other child involved.[3]

The following month Child F confided in her parents that she had had sexual intercourse at the school. Her parents took her to the GP who examined her and identified an injury which might have been caused by sexual activity. Child F's mother raised the matter with the school's headmaster. The sequence of events that followed this is disputed, but it is clear that several days passed before a safeguarding referral was made to Hampshire Children's Services Department. The report notes that:

> During that time further information came to light and concerns emerged that the sexual activity had been non-consensual, so that there was effectively an allegation of rape.[4]

The ensuing police investigation continued over several months and led to further investigations.

---

3 *Ibid.*, para 4.2.6.
4 *Ibid.*, para 4.2.8.

In September 2011, the pupil who had committed the alleged rape was arrested and suspended from the school. Later in the month, a second police investigation commenced after the school reported non-consensual sexual activity between Child F and another male pupil.

There was little evidence of alertness to the need to consider informing and involving parents.

Unsatisfactory responses

The serious case review concluded that the responses of school staff to Child F's sexual and emotional vulnerabilities were 'unsatisfactory' and highlighted six specific failures:

- There is no evidence of any school staff, including those with designated special responsibilities, demonstrating an adequate awareness of safeguarding issues in relation to Child F – the school had child protection policies but did not follow them and evidence of cause for concern was repeatedly set aside;
- Parents were not always informed of reported serious incidents and allegations;
- Other agencies were not always appropriately contacted – school staff initiated investigations which should have been immediately referred to agencies with statutory responsibilities;
- There was no consistent recognition that sexual activity between young people might raise safeguarding concerns, even in this context of young people with a range of vulnerabilities;
- Some staff displayed, at best, confusion over confidentiality. 'Confidentiality' was used inappropriately to excuse failures to act;
- Record-keeping was poor - the school effectively used no reliable systems for keeping formal records of incidents, meetings, communications and advice to staff in respect of dealing with or about Child F, or other young people.[5]

The review also noted that:

There was little evidence of alertness to the need to consider informing and involving parents, when it was known that Child F had been involved in sexual activity after the consultation with the school's GP.[6]

5 *Ibid.*, para 6.1.15.
6 *Ibid.*, para 6.1.17.

CHAPTER 8

Bristol (2016)

'A confused and confusing stance in national policy about adolescent sexual activity, leaves professionals and managers struggling to recognise and distinguish between sexual abuse, sexual exploitation and/or underage sexual activity; this risks leaving some children at continued risk of exploitation in the mistaken belief they are involved in consensual activity.'[1]

OVERVIEW

This serious case review was commissioned jointly by Bristol and an unnamed local safeguarding children board in August 2014. It concerned the sexual exploitation of a number of children in Bristol between December 2012 and May 2014. The subsequent police investigations known as Brooke 1 and Brooke 2 resulted in the successful prosecution of 15 offenders, all of whom received significant sentences for their crimes.

There was a marked difference in the way the children in Brooke 1 and 2 experienced sexual exploitation. Brooke 1 is described as 'more opportunistic in nature', while Brooke 2 involved a greater degree of premeditation and planning.

Brooke 1 focussed on offences committed between January-May 2013 at a flat in Bristol occupied by a vulnerable 16 year-old girl. A group of Class A drug dealers, mainly aged in their early 20s, identified her home as an ideal base for drug dealing. A number of men sexually exploited the girl by paying her and selling her for sex. She later disclosed that she had been raped on two occasions.

The men also encouraged her to provide them with other young victims. Other children (including three other victims, aged 14 and 15) were invited to the flat by an older girl at different times and so came into contact with the offenders.

1 Jenny Myers and Edi Carmi, *The Brooke Serious Case Review into Child Sexual Exploitation: Identifying the strengths and gaps in the multi-agency responses to child sexual exploitation in order to learn and improve*, Final Report, Bristol Safeguarding Children Board, March 2016, Finding 2, para 7.2.

Brooke 2 was concerned with allegations relating to the sexual exploitation of six vulnerable children by young men aged between 18-23, dating back to early 2012. The subsequent trial considered 35 offences, which had been committed at various locations and at different times within the Bristol area. The offences comprised of allegations of rape, arranging payment for sexual services of a child, sexual activity with a child under the age of 16 and trafficking for sexual purposes.

ANALYSIS

In a section on the period before wider sexual exploitation in Bristol was recognised (October 2011-December 2012), the serious case review notes that various reports were made to the police and children's social care by Barnardo's Against Sexual Exploitation (BASE) and others about some of the children being involved in sexual activities and sexual abuse concerns. However, it comments that:

> In general professionals from all the key agencies were slow to recognise during this time period that sexual exploitation of any of the children was taking place. They did not listen enough to the concerns of parents who were describing it and seemed to view it as consensual underage sexual activity.[2]

The police were disinclined to investigate allegations of sexual assaults on young people on the basis that it was unlikely that a prosecution would succeed. The report reveals that:

> For one child an original complaint to Avon and Somerset police of sexual assault, made in August 2012, was not followed up for five months and even then it was done so superficially. The young person at the time was aged 11 and it would seem that had investigating police officers looked into it, that there was video and other social media evidence of her assault. The Police officer reported to the lead reviewers that they felt the decision not to do anything was heavily influenced by the police view that a successful prosecution was unlikely.[3]

Relaxed attitudes towards underage sex

The report reveals a climate in which sexual activity among young people under the age of consent was regarded as normal and not worthy of note.

---

2 *Ibid.*, para 6.3.1.

3 *Ibid.*, para 6.3.3.

Medical practitioners and other health professionals consequently took a relaxed approach:

> All of the girls began to be seen during this time period by both their own GP practices and other local sexual health providers, though at the time no patterns or links were made and information about early prescribing of contraception, and other concerning sexual health related matters, were not viewed as concerning or worth sharing.[4]

One GP did make a referral to children's social care at the end of 2012 in connection with concerns about the sexual health of a 13 year-old and information that the parent had shared with him. However, it had taken months to reach this stage in spite of a history of sexual health problems and concerns about the girl's emotional health following an earlier sexual assault.[5]

In some cases, the readiness of GPs and other health workers to provide contraception to young people under the age of consent was facilitating ongoing sexual exploitation. For example:

> One Brooke perpetrator aged 18 was involved with a 12 year old child in this period, but both the child and her parent perceived this man to be under the age of 16 years old himself, as well as being in a relationship with the girl concerned. Professionals were unaware of this relationship and when the GP in Bristol became aware she was in a sexual relationship she was then aged thirteen years old. Contraception was provided, as it was understood to be a consensual relationship with a 14 year old boy. At the time she was accompanied to the GP by a family member, which may have influenced the view that she was living in a protective environment and able to consent. In discussion with the lead reviewers the health staff at the GP practice acknowledged that actually it was unusual for a 13 year old girl to seek contraception, or emergency contraception and that it should have triggered more professional curiosity and action.[6]

Routine treatment

During the period immediately preceding the launch of the two Brooke investigations, there was an increase in the incidence of allegations and

4 *Ibid.*, para 6.3.5.
5 *Ibid.*, para 6.3.7.
6 *Ibid.*, para 6.3.6.

reports to police involving the victims in these two cases. This eventually led to police recognition of organised sexual exploitation in Bristol. But in the meantime, the victims of abuse were continuing to be routinely treated for sexually transmitted infections and provided with contraception without child protection concerns being aroused. The report states:

Because of this perception of consensual sexual activity, referrals were not always made to police and children's social care.

> The girls in the case review continued to be seen numerous times by doctors and sexual health providers all presenting with similar complaints of heavy bleeding, abdominal pains, urinary tract infections and needing tests for sexually transmitted diseases alongside requesting contraception, pregnancy tests and emergency contraception. Often these visits coincided either with the girls just about to go missing or coming back from being missing.[7]

The serious case review found that:

> A confused and confusing stance in national policy about adolescent sexual activity, leaves professionals and managers struggling to recognise and distinguish between sexual abuse, sexual exploitation and/or underage sexual activity; this risks leaving some children at continued risk of exploitation in the mistaken belief they are involved in consensual activity.[8]

The report goes on to refer to 'an underlying complexity related to the contradictions within our culture about teenage sexuality, as well as in the way the law is interpreted'.[9] With hindsight, members of the review team were able to identify 'a large number of missed opportunities to recognise that the children were at risk of significant harm through sexual abuse, and that in some cases this abuse constituted sexual exploitation'. However, at the time, the abuse was undetected and 'instead the children were considered to be involved in consensual (and in most instances, under age i.e. under the age of 16) sexual activity':[10]

> Because of this perception of consensual sexual activity, referrals were not always

7 *Ibid.*, para 6.4.14.
8 *Ibid.*, Finding 2, para 7.2.
9 *Ibid.*, para 7.2.1.
10 *Ibid.*, para 7.2.2,

made to police and children's social care, and when they were made, this did not always lead to a child protection response.[11]

'Lifestyle choices'

Parents reported that professionals were inclined to blame the girls themselves for what was happening. One set of parents commented: 'People would say she brought it all on herself,' while the parent of a girl who had been raped twice was told by an investigating police officer that she was 'making lifestyle choices'.[12]

But the professionals were not alone in their failure to identify when abuse was occurring. The report notes a further 'complicating factor' in that 'the children themselves also did not see themselves as being sexually abused or exploited ***at the time***' (emphasis in original). One of the children told the review team that 'the behaviour became normal and that she didn't know that relationships with males could be any different'.[13]

The report attributes an inconsistency in the identification of child sexual abuse to 'the wider societal mixed messages about [the] sexual activity of children'. The problem was not limited to any one of the children considered by the review team, but was widespread.[14] The review team found that detecting the sexual abuse of older children was even more challenging than with younger ones. With reference to guidance from the Home Office and the Crown Prosecution Service, the serious case review observes that 'there is no intention to prosecute teenagers under the age of 16 where both mutually agree to sexual activity and where they are of a similar age and are judged to have capacity to make such a decision'. But the review goes on to demonstrate how the policy of turning a blind eye to the law on the age of consent presents a major dilemma to professionals. The report states:

> This means that professionals with knowledge of such sexual activity have to try to establish both whether consent is involved, the age and power difference between those involved in the relationship and their mental capacity to make such decisions. Such individual professional judgments will be variable and will be highly dependent on the accounts provided by the child her/himself.[15]

11 *Ibid.*, para 7.2.3.
12 *Ibid.*, para 7.2.7.
13 *Ibid.*, para 7.2.5.
14 *Ibid.*, para 7.2.8.
15 *Ibid.*, para 7.2.11.

Another problem highlighted by the report is that the young people themselves cannot be relied upon to give an honest and accurate account of the nature of the relationships in which they are engaged:

> It is even more difficult to engage children to talk about their sexual activity if/when they know it is illegal. Moreover children involved in underage sexual activity are likely to be subject to pressure not to disclose the age of sexual partners, often referring to them as 'boyfriends', even though they are adult males, (if they know their actual age themselves), nor the extent of, or lack of, informed consent. It was striking in this cohort of victims that discussions with doctors and nurses regarding contraception or sexual health consistently involved (misleading) accounts of sexual partners of just a year or two older than themselves.[16]

Confusion surrounding confidentiality

The serious case review also demonstrates how confidentiality policies can militate against child protection procedures. It notes that:

> Whilst GPs are usually provided with all information about their patients accessing health services, this is not true for sexual health services. This means that no one health practitioner has knowledge of what was being prescribed for each young person or the frequency or nature of health presentations. A significant factor, appears to be the wider implications of information sharing protocols and patient confidentiality within sexual health services, arising from the need to encourage children to seek help and the fear they may not do so if their family GP is informed. There is also stringent legislation that creates a barrier to sharing sexual health information.[17]

Yet the victims of child sexual exploitation appealed to professionals to be more inquisitive and not to shrink from sharing information. One girl told the review team:

> Know it is really embarrassing to talk about sexual things to adults, especially if those sexual experiences have hurt you. We want professionals, including sexual health nurses and GPs to ask us better questions, be more inquisitive and if necessary to examine us when we ask for morning after pills, or seem very

16 *Ibid.*, para 7.2.12.

17 *Ibid.*, para 7.5.3.

young for contraception. We may have hidden bruises and marks, so do not take everything we say at face value. Don't get so hung up on confidentiality, sometimes you do need to share what we have said.[18]

'Don't get so hung up on confidentiality, sometimes you do need to share what we have said.'

Another young person told the lead reviewers that she was amazed that at the age of 13 she was given the morning-after pill by her GP:

> She said that at the time she wanted to say something more about what was happening but felt everything she said was taken at face value, on another occasion she says she had bruises and scratches on her thighs (she had been raped) but was never examined, again she wanted someone to be more curious.[19]

Not without reason does the report state that: 'The confusion created by national guidance on patient confidentiality, data protection and legal rights appears to get in the way of keeping child safeguarding as the most paramount consideration.'[20]

Indeed, confusion is a recurring theme in the Bristol serious case review. The report correctly observes:

> The current political and media focus on sexual exploitation is likely to trigger an increased recognition of this extremely harmful abuse of children. However, there remains an underlying confusion for practitioners in distinguishing between underage but consensual sexual activity between peers and child sexual abuse and sexual exploitation. Such confusion is rooted in the complex and contradictory cultural, legal and moral norms around sexuality, and in particular teenage sexual experimentation.[21]

Such confusion and such contradictions need to be honestly faced and addressed if we are to provide children and young people with adequate protection from child sexual exploitation.

18 *Ibid.*, para 4.2.
19 *Ibid.*, para 7.7.17
20 *Ibid.*, para 8.1.9.
21 *Ibid.*, para 7.2.18.

PART 2
HOW PUBLIC POLICY IS PLACING CHILDREN AND YOUNG PEOPLE AT RISK

> *'The challenge of tackling child sexual exploitation also requires agencies and individuals to think about issues such as the proper limits for sexual activity involving children, as well as the degree to which children are developing their own rights and self-direction (what academics call 'agency'). These are not easy issues and it would be naive to imagine there is complete unanimity in our society at this current time.'*[1]

The evidence from the serious case reviews is striking. Relaxed attitudes towards underage sex led to what can only be described as a paralysis in child protection agencies as far apart as Rochdale in the north, Torbay in the south, Thurrock in the east and Liverpool in the west.

The fact that the same failures have occurred in such diverse parts of the country suggests an underlying problem that runs much deeper than can be accounted for by the incompetence of individual officers or inadequate systems at the local level. The root of the malaise would appear not to be primarily personal and systemic, but rather social, cultural and moral.

In seven of the eight regions we have considered, cases of child sexual exploitation were deemed to have reached a sufficient level of severity to demand a serious case review and, in Rotherham, an independent inquiry. But the sexual exploitation of children is by no means confined to a relatively small number of districts. Indeed, a report published by the House of Commons Communities and Local Government Committee in the wake of Professor Jay's report on Rotherham, reached 'the alarming conclusion...that Rotherham was not an outlier and that there is a

1 Professor John Drew CBE, *Drew Review - An independent review of South Yorkshire Police's handling of child sexual exploitation 1997-2016*, March 2016, p.18.

widespread problem of organised child sexual exploitation in England'.[2]

In this section we shall examine some of the factors that have created a climate in which professionals charged with child protection and law enforcement have become negligent, while child sexual exploitation has continued to grow in prevalence.

2 House of Commons Communities and Local Government Committee, *Child sexual exploitation in Rotherham: some issues for local government*, Third Report of Session 2014-15, November 2014, para 17.

CHAPTER 9
The normalisation of underage sex

'If all cases of underage sex are now to be reported, the agencies will be snowed under and suffocated in a month! The problem is that child protection agencies, schools and sexual health projects have not taken underage sex seriously.

'Also liberal people in sexual health programmes, reacting against right-wing religious lobbies, have failed to address issues of coercion and macho sexism even among similar-aged teenagers, and act as if everyone was giving freely informed consent at 12, 13 or 14. So numerous cases of coerced sex have been missed by well-meaning people.'[1]

The independent inquiry and serious case reviews considered in the previous section demonstrate a widespread acceptance, and even expectation, that children under the age of 16 will be sexually active. The assumption that many victims of sexual exploitation were engaging in consensual relationships was a major factor in the failure of child protection agencies to protect them.

The House of Commons Home Affairs Committee reported that:

> The lack of curiosity about localised grooming and its manifestations shown by all official agencies has been a running theme in our inquiry. We have been told that in the cases of Rotherham and Rochdale, professionals did not recognise the existence of the exploitation, were not aware of the scale of the abuse, were not sharing information that, had it been brought together in one place, would have disclosed a pattern of widespread abuse. This is partly due to the assumptions around the fact that victims were engaging in consensual relationships and the inability to engage with the victims.[2]

1 Dr Sarah Nelson, University of Edinburgh, letter to *Community Care*, 19-25 August 2004.

2 House of Commons Home Affairs Committee, *Child sexual exploitation and the response to localised grooming*, Volume 1, Second Report of Session 2013–14, para 53, (emphasis added).

Social and cultural attitudes

In the light of three separate reports into child sexual exploitation, Ofsted's annual report for social care in 2013-14 stated that: 'Too often, children and young people who had been sexually exploited were wrongly labelled as "promiscuous" or considered to have made a "lifestyle choice" that entailed engaging in risky behaviour.'[3]

The Peterborough Safeguarding Children Board set child sexual exploitation in the region within a particular cultural context. It referred to:

> The culture of conceptualising young people as 'young adults' capable and with the freedom to make 'unwise decisions' and the notion that they were choosing to have abusive relationships. Therefore, the lack of visibility of conceptualising young people as victims of [child sexual exploitation] with complex needs.[4]

Lucy Allan, MP for Telford, which has the highest recorded rate of child sex offences in the country, told the House of Commons that there needs be 'a much better understanding of social and cultural attitudes' towards girls and young women. She expressed concern that an acceptance of underage sex had blinded professionals to the reality that children were suffering as the victims of sexual exploitation. She observed:

> Too often, assumptions were made that the young girls were making choices to have regular underage sex. We see, for example, GPs handing out morning-after pills to the same young girls week after week, without asking questions, simply assuming that it is a choice the girls are making. It is wrong to blame children as young as 12 for 'indulging in risky behaviour' or label them as sexually promiscuous. That is completely wrong.[5]

Whether the young people were perceived to be engaging in 'consensual relationships' (the Home Affairs Committee), 'promiscuous'/'risky behaviour' (Ofsted), 'choosing to have abusive relationships' (Peterborough Safeguarding Children Board), or 'making choices to have regular underage sex' (Lucy Allan MP), the agencies charged with ensuring their

---

3 Ofsted, *The report of Her Majesty's Chief Inspector of Education, Children's Services and Skills 2013–14: Social Care*, 2015, para 56.

4 Ceryl Teleri Davies, *An overview of the multi-agency response to child sexual exploitation in Peterborough*, Peterborough Safeguarding Children Board, June 2016, p.8.

5 Westminster Hall Debate, *Child Sexual Exploitation: Telford*, House of Commons Hansard, 25 October 2016, col 81WH.

protection failed to intervene. Even where the girls concerned were under the age of 16 and therefore below the age of consent to sexual intercourse, the statutory authorities remained complacent and did not consider it their role to become involved.

In the following chapters, we shall consider the factors that lay behind this inactivity and seek to identify the roots of a culture in which underage sex has come to be regarded as normal.

CHAPTER 10

Undermining the age of consent

'[O]ne fact was glaringly clear: most of the girls involved were below the age of consent, so what was happening was obviously against the law.

But that apparently didn't strike the authorities with any force, partly because the age of consent has so often come to be regarded as virtually irrelevant. It started out, some years ago, as a kind of pragmatic exercise in damage limitation: many girls did have sex below the age of 16, and the concern of the authorities was not to dissuade them from having sex – which it deemed a lost cause – but to prevent them from getting pregnant. Now, pragmatism has effectively hardened into a form of reckless abandonment.'[1]

Throughout the United Kingdom, the age of consent to sexual activity is 16. In the words of the Crown Prosecution Service (CPS) guidelines, 'any sexual activity involving consenting children under 16 is unlawful'.[2] The CPS also states that:

> The age of consent is 16. Because children can and do abuse and exploit other children, [the Sexual Offences Act 2003] makes it an offence for children under 16 to engage in sexual activity, to protect children who are victims.[3]

However, in its guidance on sexual offences by youths, the CPS raises the expectation that consensual sexual activity involving two teenagers where one or both parties are under the age of 16 will not be prosecuted. The guidance states:

> It should be noted that where both parties to sexual activity are under 16, then

1 Jenny McCartney, 'Teenage girls suffer as we look the other way', *Sunday Telegraph*, 30 September 2012.

2 Crown Prosecution Service, *Legal Guidance on Rape and Sexual Offences: Chapter 2, http://www.cps.gov.uk/legal/p_to_r/rape_and_sexual_offences/soa_2003_and_soa_1956/* Accessed 15 February 2017.

3 Crown Prosecution Service, *Factsheet on Sexual Offences http://www.cps.gov.uk/news/fact_sheets/sexual_offences/* Accessed 15 February 2017.

they may both have committed a criminal offence. However, the overriding purpose of the legislation is to protect children and it was not Parliament's intention to punish children unnecessarily or for the criminal law to intervene where it was wholly inappropriate. Consensual sexual activity between, for example, a 14 or 15 year-old and a teenage partner would not normally require criminal proceedings in the absence of aggravating features. The relevant considerations include:

- the respective ages of the parties;
- the existence and nature of any relationship;
- their level of maturity;
- whether any duty of care existed;
- whether there was a serious element of exploitation.[4]

Advice to young people

It is this guidance that enables Brook to advise young people:

> If you are under 16 and you are having sex, it is less likely that you will get into trouble if there is not a large age difference between you and your partner, you both consent (i.e are happy to have sex) and there's no evidence of any exploitation.[5]

Or, more crudely, Warwickshire County Council's *Respect Yourself* website for young people offers the following response to the questions: 'Why do you have to be 16 to have sex? What if you want it now?':

> In the UK 16 is the age of consent – this is the age the law sees us as being mature enough to decide and agree to sex for ourselves. The law is there to protect children and young people from paedophiles. However, this creates a problem as everyone matures at different ages and you are the only one who really knows if and when you are ready.[6]

In its section on 'Sex and the law', the same website states:

---

4 Crown Prosecution Service, *Legal Guidance on Rape and Sexual Offences: Chapter 11. http://www.cps.gov.uk/legal/p_to_r/rape_and_sexual_offences/youths/* Accessed 15 February 2017.

5 Brook, *Sex, relationships and your rights. https://www.brook.org.uk/your-life/sex-relationships-and-your-rights* Accessed 15 February 2017.

6 Warwickshire County Council, *Respect Yourself* website, 'Your Questions' *http://respectyourself.info/your-questions/#faq596 Accessed 15 February 2017.*

'The only person who can tell you you're ready – is you – not your partner, not your folks not your friends and ultimately not a policeman.'
Warwickshire County Council

When you're considering getting naked with someone you really fancy probably one of the last things on your mind is the law – obviously there are the rape laws when a person forces someone to have sex – however, when you're both horny and fancy the pants off each other, what's the law got to do with it?...

[I]n this country there is a legal age limit as to when you are allowed to have sex: 16 years old – this is called the age of consent. The law says that you are not old enough or mature enough to make that decision for yourself as you are still legally a child, so it makes that decision for you and it automatically says No...

As a law it's pretty hard to enforce anyway. It's not like we have the 'Sex Police' that hide under every teenager's bed ready to jump out and get you. In actual fact the law is not there to stop underage teens from having sex together, it's there for protection, to prevent paedophiles... Unfortunately by putting an age limit on things we don't take into consideration people's maturity...

The fact is you won't go to bed the night before your 16th birthday thinking I'm not ready yet and then next day blow out your candles and POW – suddenly you're ready! The only person who can tell you you're ready – is you – not your partner, not your folks not your friends and ultimately not a policeman.[7]

Members of the judiciary may not customarily employ the language found on the *Respect Yourself* website, but such views are certainly represented on the Bench. Passing judgment in a rare instance where a case of consensual teenage sex was brought to court, Judge Sylvia de Bertodano severely criticised the CPS:

I don't know what the world has come to when I am asked to deal, in a serious criminal court, with two teenagers who got drunk and had sex... These sort of cases have no place in this kind of court.[8]

7 Warwickshire County Council, *op. cit.*, 'Sex and The Law'. *http://respectyourself.info/sex/sex-and-the-law/ Accessed 15 February 2017.*

8 'Judge in underage sex case says she feels "extremely sorry" for defendant', *Daily Telegraph*, 10 April 2015.

Young people are frequently being given the impression that engaging in sexual activity under the age of 16 is no big deal. Provided it is consensual and so long as the age gap is not too wide, the authorities are likely to turn a blind eye and the risk of prosecution is extremely low.

Such messages are leaving young teenage girls vulnerable to approaches from predatory males who shower them with gifts and attention and present themselves as 'boyfriends', frequently claiming to be younger than they really are.

Sexual activity involving under-13s

On the one hand, the legal age of consent remains 16, while on the other hand, children under the age of 16 are deemed capable of consenting to sexual activity with another child or young person of a similar age. However, the CPS is clear that under the Sexual Offences Act 2003, 'Any sexual intercourse with a child under 13 will be treated as rape'.[9]

In her inspection report regarding Rotherham Metropolitan Borough Council, Louise Casey unambiguously stated:

> A child under 13 does not, under any circumstances, have legal capacity to consent to any form of sexual activity. Penetration of any kind would amount to rape which is punishable by up to life imprisonment.[10]

However, even here the CPS guidance is less than categorical and allows for the possibility of consensual sexual activity on the part of children under the age of 13:

> If the sexual act or activity was in fact genuinely consensual and the youth and the child under 13 concerned are fairly close in age and development, a prosecution is unlikely to be appropriate. Action falling short of prosecution may be appropriate. In such cases, the parents and/or welfare agencies may be able to deal with the situation informally. There is a fine line between sexual experimentation and offending and in general, children under the age of 13 should not be criminalised for sexual behaviour in the absence of coercion, exploitation or abuse of trust.[11]

Not only is there a reluctance to initiate criminal proceedings where

9 Crown Prosecution Service, *Factsheet on Sexual Offences*, op. cit.

10 Louise Casey, *Report of Inspection of Rotherham Metropolitan Borough Council*, February 2015, p.57.

11 Crown Prosecution Service, *Legal Guidance on Rape and Sexual Offences: Chapter 11*, op. cit.

sexual activity involving children and young people under the legal age of consent is deemed to be consensual, but there is even a disinclination to view unlawful sex as a safeguarding issue in some circumstances.

In Bristol, 'knowledge by health professionals of recurrent sexual health problems to a girl under the age of 13 years, even in the context of previous sexual abuse, did not lead to consistent reporting of such concerns to CYPS [Children and Young People's Services]'.[12]

The Hampshire serious case review commented that:

> The intervention of child protection agencies in situations involving sexual activity between children can require difficult professional judgments. Some situations are statutorily clear – for example, a child under the age of 13 cannot consent to sexual activity. But it will not necessarily be appropriate to initiate safeguarding procedures where sexual activity involving children and young people below the age of legal consent (16 years) comes to notice. In our society generally the age at which children become sexually active has steadily dropped. It is important to distinguish between consensual sexual activity between children of a similar age (where at least one is below the age of consent), and sexual activity involving a power imbalance, or some form of coercion or exploitation. It may also be difficult to be sure that what has or has been alleged to have taken place definitely does have a sexual component.[13]

That 'in our society generally the age at which children become sexually active has steadily dropped' is noted with complacency as a mere matter of fact. It is almost as if the authors believe that the application of the law must be modified in order to reflect changing social trends. There does not appear to be any acknowledgement of the possibility a relaxed attitude towards the legal age of consent may have contributed to the rise in underage sex – and also to cases of child sexual exploitation.

Dr Sarah Nelson from the University of Edinburgh, a leading researcher on sexual abuse, warned about the consequences of not taking underage sex seriously well over a decade ago. She wrote:

> If all cases of underage sex are now to be reported, the agencies will be snowed under and suffocated in a month! The problem is that child protection agencies, schools and sexual health projects have not taken underage sex seriously.

12 Myers and Carmi, *The Brooke Serious Case Review*, op. cit., para 7.2.10.
13 Harrington and Whyte, *The safeguarding implications*, op. cit., para 7.2.1.

> Also liberal people in sexual health programmes, reacting against right-wing religious lobbies, have failed to address issues of coercion and macho sexism even among similar-aged teenagers, and act as if everyone was giving freely informed consent at 12, 13 or 14. So numerous cases of coerced sex have been missed by well-meaning people.[14]

The Independent Chair of the Oxfordshire Safeguarding Children Board noted that: 'There were misguided interpretations of the law around consent, and an apparent tolerance of (or failure to be alarmed by) unlawful sexual activity.'[15] It is evident that such attitudes are widespread and that where they are present they are facilitating child sexual exploitation and abuse and hindering child protection. The Oxfordshire report accordingly recommends that:

> Relevant government departments should consider the impact of current guidance on consent to ensure what seems to be the ever-lower age at which a child can be deemed to consent (for example to treatment) and attitudes to underage sex are not making it easier for perpetrators to succeed.[16]

---

14 Sarah Nelson, *Community Care*, op. cit.

15 Blyth, Statement to Press Conference, *op. cit.*; Bedford, *Serious Case Review*, op. cit., para 8.4.

16 Bedford, *Serious Case Review*, *op. cit.*, para 9.14.

CHAPTER 11

The confidential provision of contraception to under-16s

'The girls lost the ability to consent or make their own decisions due to grooming. The law around consent was not properly understood, and this was compounded by contraception being prescribed (albeit legally) long before the law states children are legally able to have sex. There was a professional tolerance to knowing young teenagers were having sex with adults.'[1]

For over 40 years it has been Department of Health policy to permit the confidential provision of contraception to young people under the age of 16 without the knowledge or consent of their parents.[2] This policy was challenged during the early 1980s by Victoria Gillick. After the High Court initially upheld the Department's policy, the Court of Appeal ruled in Mrs Gillick's favour, only for the House of Lords to subsequently overturn the Court of Appeal's decision by a margin of three to two in 1985. However, in delivering their judgment, the law lords were insistent that under all normal circumstances the child's parents should be informed and be in agreement with the supply of contraceptive treatment to an underage girl. Lord Scarman ruled:

> ...a doctor is only in exceptional circumstances to prescribe contraception to a young person under the age of 16 without the knowledge and consent of a parent... Only in exceptional cases does the guidance contemplate [a doctor] exercising his clinical judgement without the parents' knowledge and consent.[3]

Lord Fraser concurred:

> Nobody doubts, certainly I do not doubt, that in the overwhelming majority of cases the best judges of a child's welfare are his or her parents. Nor do I doubt

1 Maggie Blyth, *Child Sexual Exploitation: Making a Difference*, Oxfordshire Safeguarding Children Board, June 2015, p.8.

2 Department of Health and Social Security, *Family Planning Services*, Memorandum of Guidance, May 1974.

3 Gillick v West Norfolk and Wisbech Area Health Authority and another - [1985] 3 All ER 402.

> that any important medical treatment of a child under 16 would normally only be carried out with the parents' approval. That is why it would and should be most unusual for a doctor to advise a child without the knowledge and consent of parents on contraceptive matters.[4]

Since that time, health professionals have frequently appealed to the 'Fraser criteria' to defend the confidential provision of contraception to young people under the age of 16.[5] However, as we noted in chapter 1, Lord Fraser added that his criteria:

> ought not to be regarded as a licence for doctors to disregard the wishes of parents on this matter whenever they find it convenient to do so. Any doctor who behaves in such a way would, in my opinion, be failing to discharge his professional responsibilities, and I would expect him to be disciplined by his own professional body accordingly.[6]

In 1985, few could have foreseen the scale on which contraception and emergency hormonal birth control (the 'morning-after pill') would be made available to growing numbers of children, not only through their GP or a sexual health clinic, but also from high street pharmacies and clinics operating on school premises. A report published in 2007 found that three-fifths of Primary Care Trusts in England were prepared under some circumstances to insist on underage provision of emergency hormonal birth control as a condition of granting a pharmacy licence.[7]

The duty of confidentiality

The Department of Health's current guidance to health professionals on contraception, sexual and reproductive health services (including abortion) for under-16s places a strong emphasis on 'the duty of confidentiality'. Issued in July 2004, the document states that:

> All services providing advice and treatment on contraception, sexual and reproductive health should produce an explicit confidentiality policy which... makes clear that young people have the same right to confidentiality as adults.[8]

---

4 *Ibid.*

5 See p. 19.

6 *Ibid.*

7 Norman Wells and Helena Hayward, *Waking Up to the Morning-After Pill*, Family Education Trust, 2007.

8 Department of Health, *Best practice guidance for doctors and other health professionals on the provision of advice and treatment to young people under 16 on contraception, sexual and reproductive health*, July 2004.

The guidance specifies that such confidentiality policies 'should be prominently advertised, in partnership with education, youth and community services'. Unless there is 'a risk to the health, safety or welfare of a young person or others which is so serious as to outweigh the young person's right to privacy', any deliberate breach of confidentiality is to be treated as a serious disciplinary matter.

The guidance lists several issues which it is considered 'good practice' for doctors and health professionals to discuss with a young person to help him/her to make an 'informed choice', but at no point is any reference made to the law on the age of consent. Neither is there any acknowledgement of the law lords' ruling that contraceptive provision to underage girls without parental knowledge or consent should be 'most unusual' and occur 'only in exceptional circumstances'. The impression is given throughout that young people are free to make an 'informed choice' about engaging in an unlawful sexual relationship under the age of 16.

Sexual Offences Act 2003

The only reference to statute in the Department of Health guidance appears in a section designed to assure health professionals that 'the Sexual Offences Act 2003 does not affect the ability of health professionals and others working with young people to provide confidential advice or treatment on contraception, sexual and reproductive health to young people under 16'.[9]

Under the terms of the Act, health professionals, teachers, Connexions Personal Advisers, youth workers, social practitioners, parents and anyone else acting to protect a child, are deemed to be 'not guilty of aiding, abetting or counselling a sexual offence against a child where they are acting for the purpose of:

- 'protecting a child from pregnancy or sexually transmitted infection,
- 'protecting the physical safety of a child,
- 'promoting a child's emotional well-being by the giving of advice.'

The confidential provision of contraception to young people under the legal age of consent is thus justified on the basis that it may help the child to avoid becoming pregnant or contracting a sexually transmitted infection.

9 *Ibid.*

Open access and its consequences

In its local government briefing on contraceptive services, the National Institute for Health and Care Excellence (NICE) accordingly recommends that access should 'be open to young people aged under 16 without a parent or carer' and specifies that its guidance 'includes everyone under age 16 who is competent to consent to contraceptive treatment'.[10]

According to a study published in the *Journal of Family Planning and Reproductive Health Care*, there was a 50 per cent increase in the number of girls and young women aged 12-18 prescribed the contraceptive pill during the first decade of the new millennium. In 2011, 19 per cent of female adolescents received a prescription for hormonal contraceptives, compared with 13.7 per cent in 2002. This amounts to one in 20 females aged 12-18 now taking the contraceptive pill.[11]

Figures from NHS Digital show that young people under the age of 16 made contact with dedicated Sexual and Reproductive Health (SRH) services on 70,900 occasions in 2015/16 and requested a total of 132,400 activities. By far the majority of these activities related to contraception (64,400) and sexual health advice (43,200). Eight per cent of 15 year-old girls had at least one contact with SRH services, which include family planning services, community contraception clinics, integrated Genito-urinary medicine (GUM) and SRH clinics, and young people's services such as those operated by Brook. These services were also accessed by 13,700 young people aged 13-14, and by several hundred children under the age of 13. These statistics are limited to dedicated SRH services and do not include those young people under 16 who obtained contraception or sexual health advice from other sources such as GPs or local pharmacies.[12]

C-Card schemes

Over recent years, C-Card schemes offering free condoms to young people have been in operation in different parts of the country. Public Health England, an executive agency of the Department of Health, in association with Brook, has published guidance in the 'why, what

10 NICE, *Contraceptive Services: Local government briefing* [LGB17], March 2014. *https://www.nice.org.uk/advice/lgb17/chapter/what-nice-says* Accessed 15 February 2017.

11 A Rashed *et al*, 'Trends and patterns of hormonal contraceptive prescribing for adolescents in primary care in the UK', *Journal of Family Planning and Reproductive Health Care*, 2015; 41:216-222.

12 NHS Digital, Sexual and Reproductive Health Services, England - 2015-16, 19 October 2016 *http://www.content.digital.nhs.uk/catalogue/PUB21969* Accessed 18 February 2017.

and how' of condom distribution schemes. The guidance states that, 'The scheme provides a welcoming, inclusive, clear, friendly, safe, non-judgemental service.'[13]

Although some schemes have a lower age limit (typically 13 or 14), the guidance states that:

> Brook recommends that young people ***of all ages*** should be able to access the scheme, and that professionals must be trained and supported to decide whether the young person can access condoms based on an assessment of their safety and their competence to consent.[14]

The 'summary of the features of a good C-Card scheme' includes the provision that 'young people can access the service on their own at any age'.[15]

Even where C-Card schemes have a lower age limit, many health authorities do not rule out providing condoms to children below the stated minimum age. For example, the guidance for the Norfolk and Waveney C-Card scheme states:

> Young people aged under 13 are unable to sign up to the C-Card scheme. If a young person under 13 is sexually active the C-Card practitioner should follow their own Safeguarding Children procedures and protocols. If the C-Card practitioner judges it appropriate to supply the young person with condoms, then they can do so, but not as part of the C-Card scheme and these actions should be recorded.[16]

Some other schemes direct enquirers under the minimum age to their GP or to a sexual health clinic.

Sex under 13?

Shortly after the Sexual Offences Act 2003 came into force with its new legal provisions aimed at providing additional protection for children under the age of 13, the Sex Education Forum swiftly issued a briefing to emphasise that, 'The Act **does not limit children's right to sex and**

13 Public Health England and Brook, *C-Card condom distribution schemes – why, what and how*, July 2014, p.19.

14 *Ibid.*, p.6 (emphasis added).

15 *Ibid.*, p.19.

16 East Coast Community Healthcare Sexual Health Promotion Unit, *Norfolk and Waveney Your C-Card (Condom Card) Scheme Guidance*, January 2015, para 4.1.2.

relationships education and sexual health support and advice.'

The Forum, which claims to be 'the national authority on sex and relationships education', stressed that: 'Young people under 16, including those under 13, **can continue to seek sexual health and contraceptive information, advice or treatment in confidence.**'[17]

One of the leading organisations within the Sex Education Forum, the *fpa*, is similarly insistent on the right of children under the age of 13 to confidential contraceptive advice and treatment. The *fpa*'s policy on Under-16s and confidentiality states that:

> FPA is committed to the principle that under-16s – including those under 13 – should be able to get confidential sexual health advice and treatment, and we believe that professionals working with young people must protect their right to confidentiality in all but the most exceptional cases...
>
> Both the law and professional guidance are clear that young people, including those under 13, are entitled to confidentiality when accessing sexual health services. Where young people are using sexual health services, it is crucial that professionals do not confuse child protection issues with the normal sexual development of young people...
>
> Furthermore, when the Sexual Offences Act came into force on 1 May 2004, the Home Office published an explanatory leaflet for professionals which states that 'Although the age of consent remains at 16, the law is not intended to prosecute mutually agreed teenage sexual activity between two young people of a similar age, unless it involves abuse or exploitation. Young people, including those under 13, will continue to have the right to confidential advice on contraception, condoms, pregnancy and abortion.'[18]

In its statement, on 'Sexual Wellbeing and Pleasure', the *fpa* asserts its commitment to 'promoting greater recognition and acceptance of the variety of ways people express their sexuality'. It goes on to encourage 'recognition and acceptance of everyone's right to express and enjoy their sexuality regardless of ability, *age*, gender, race, sexual orientation, religion

---

17 Sex Education Forum briefing on the Sexual Offences Act 2003, June 2004 (emphasis in original). *http://www.sexeducationforum.org.uk/media/6351/soact2007.pdf* Accessed 15 February 2017.

18 *fpa, Under-16s and confidentiality*, January 2011 (emphasis in original). *http://www.fpa.org.uk/sites/default/files/under-16s-and-confidentiality-policy-statement.pdf* Accessed 15 February 2017.

or culture.'[19] Clearly, in the opinion of the *fpa*, a tender age should be no barrier to sexual expression and enjoyment.

It is perhaps not surprising, then, that bodies such as the *fpa*, Brook and the British Medical Association were among the organisations which objected to a protocol for working with sexually active young people in London, which required the mandatory reporting of sexually active children below the age of 13. The document prepared by the London Child Protection Committee insisted that:

> All cases of children under the age of 13 years believed to be or have been engaged in penetrative sexual activity must be referred to Children's Social Services and the Police as a potential case of rape.[20]

The then chief executive of Brook, Jan Barlow, commented that the protocol went 'against everything we believe in'.[21] Vivienne Nathanson, Head of Ethics at the British Medical Association, held that the key issue was to ensure that children had the confidence to negotiate about whether they wanted to be sexually active, including the ability to negotiate and say no.[22]

It was perhaps a concern not to 'confuse child protection issues with the normal sexual development of young people',[23] to borrow the *fpa*'s words, that prompted the President of the Royal College of Paediatrics and Child Health, Professor David Hall, to take a relaxed attitude towards contraception provision to a 12 year-old girl involved in a sexual relationship with a 22-year-old man. That was the scenario presented to Professor Hall as he gave oral evidence before the Joint Committee on Human Rights. The Liberal Democrat MP, Norman Baker, described the scene:

> The parents are livid and want the full force of the law brought to bear on that situation. The child herself appears to be consenting and maintaining the position that she is capable of making her own decisions and the law of

19 *fpa, Sexual Wellbeing and Pleasure*, January 2011 (emphasis added). *http://www.fpa.org.uk/sites/default/files/sexual-wellbeing-policy-statement.pdf* Accessed 15 February 2017.

20 London Child Protection Committee, *Working with Sexually Active Young People under the age of 18 – a Pan-London Protocol*, April 2005.

21 Gordon Carson, 'Sexual Health: Concern that protocol will deter Children from seeking advice', *Children & Young People Now*, 31 May 2005.

22 BBC Radio 4, *Today*, 30 September 2005.

23 *fpa, Young People*, January 2011. *http://www.fpa.org.uk/sites/default/files/young-people-policy-statement.pdf* Accessed 15 February 2017.

> course says that that relationship, if it is taking place, is statutory rape which has a sentence of life imprisonment as a maximum. If the child in that situation wants contraceptive advice and contraception, how do you we *(sic)* deal with that terribly difficult situation?

Professor Hall responded:

> The advice that GPs receive...would be that as far as the young person herself is concerned you would have to make a judgment as her doctor about the right course of action. If your judgment was that she was making a mature and considered decision in coming to consult you and was asking for contraceptive advice, I think most doctors would provide that advice and treat that in confidence. If their judgment was that this girl was being manipulated and used then the terms used include 'some secrets are too big to keep'. That might be the sort of language you would use to someone you treat as a child. In the case you describe I suspect most people would feel that as far as their behaviour as a doctor was concerned, they would probably give her the advice that she was requesting because they would consider her very competent by the very act of having come to seek advice on contraception and they would consider that was how she was behaving. They would probably then ring their Medical Defence Union and say, 'Help, have I done the right thing?' I think that is probably what most of them would do.[24]

It is such attitudes that have contributed to what the former Independent Chair of the Oxfordshire Safeguarding Children Board (OSCB) described as 'a professional tolerance to knowing young teenagers were having sex with adults'.[25]

Encouraging underage sexual activity

Advocates for confidential contraceptive advice and provision for young people under the age of 16 – and even for children under the age of 13 - frequently protest that such services do not contribute to any increase in underage sexual activity.

However, the notion that harm reduction does not promote underage sexual activity defies logic. Removing, or at least limiting, unwanted

24 Joint Committee on Human Rights, Twenty-second Report of Session 2001-02, *The Case for a Human Rights Commission: Interim Report*, HL Paper 160, HC 1142, EV60.

25 Blyth, *Child Sexual Exploitation: Making a Difference*, op. cit., p.8.

consequences will always serve to encourage a desired activity. There is both anecdotal and academic evidence to show that the confidential provision of contraception to under-16s has facilitated rather than hindered teenage sexual experimentation.

'Boys push you into sex by saying you can take [the morning-after pill] the next day.'

For example, award-winning journalist and author Tanith Carey relates the experience of Sophie Lewis who lost her virginity at the age of 15 after her school recommended that she have a contraceptive implant fitted. The school also handed out condoms to pupils with few questions asked. In her late teens, Sophie 'bitterly regrets having sex so young, and firmly believes that easy access to contraception contributed to a general expectation at her secondary school that people would have sex sooner rather than later'.[26]

In a revealing article, *Sunday Times* associate editor, Eleanor Mills, related a discussion she had about the morning-after pill with a group of 16-17 year-old girls from some of Britain's top independent schools. All of them were familiar with it and half had taken it. They had first heard about it at school when they were 10 or 11. One of them recalled, 'It was all sex is fun and don't get sexually transmitted infections. They told us to use condoms.'

Another girl related: 'I took the morning-after pill when I was 13 because I was too young to even think of getting pregnant. I thought it was responsible. But boys push you into sex by saying you can take it the next day.'

Eleanor Mills commented:

> To a liberal-minded woman like me who has always seen contraception as a plank of female empowerment and freedom, to hear how these girls have been coerced into unprotected, casual sex because they can just 'go and get the morning-after pill' is shocking and upsetting. Natalie sums it up: 'Boys just think it's all right. Makes it okay for them to be very irresponsible — if it didn't exist, they would have to use other protection, have to think about us more. But we've got no comeback. It's true that if they do it to you, you can get the pill the next day. It doesn't make it right.'[27]

26 Tanith Carey, 'The children going to the school nurse for aspirin - and being given the Pill (even though they're under the age of consent and their parents don't know a thing about it)', *Daily Mail*, 10 January 2013.

27 Eleanor Mills, 'Mums are stockpiling it for their daughters, and boys think it's a licence to have sex. Is the

JO SIMPSON RELATES HER DAUGHTER'S EXPERIENCE

One of my daughters obtained contraception from the school nurse when she was only 14 after being heavily pressured by her then boyfriend. Now 18, [she] is convinced that making contraception available to pupils on school premises puts pressure on them to have sex.

If contraception had not been available at school, she feels there is no way she would have gone to the doctors or to the chemist to get contraception and therefore would not have given into the pressure that she was under. She subsequently ended the relationship with her boyfriend and has carried the regret of not waiting ever since.

I am deeply concerned that people who are strangers to our children are able to give them contraception without the consent of their parents and without our children being able to fully understand the possible consequences of what they are doing... There is no condom on earth that will protect a child from a bad reputation or a broken heart, or prevent regret. I wonder what would happen if a 14 year old went to a neighbour and obtained the same 'advice' and 'treatment'. What would happen to that neighbour?[28]

Academic research

Such anecdotal accounts are supported by the findings of academic research. Professor David Paton from Nottingham University Business School observes that standard economic models suggest a link between access to contraceptive services and the proportion of teenagers who engage in sexual activity. He concludes:

> Easier access to family planning reduces the effective cost of sexual activity and will make it more likely (at least for some teenagers) that they will engage in underage sexual activity.[29]

Professor Paton also notes evidence from the United States showing that states which have introduced mandatory parental involvement laws

morning-after pill good for girls?' *Sunday Times*, 22 July 2012.

28 Family Education Trust, *Bulletin*, Issue 145, Autumn 2011.

29 David Paton, 'Underage conceptions and abortions in England and Wales 1969-2009: the role of public policy', *Education and Health*, 2012, Vol. 30 No. 2.

have seen relative decreases in abortions to minors, a reduction in teenage sexually transmitted infections and improvements in teenage mental health.[30]

> *Easier access to family planning will make it more likely (at least for some teenagers) that they will engage in underage sexual activity.*

In a separate study published in the *Journal of Health Economics*, Professors Girma and Paton found consistent evidence that pharmacy schemes providing emergency hormonal birth control are associated with higher rates of sexually transmitted infections in teenagers.[31] More recent research has found that school condom distribution schemes have the effect of increasing both birth rates and sexually transmitted infection rates among teenagers.[32]

Contrary to the common assumption that confidential contraceptive schemes reduce teenage conception and infection rates while not encouraging teenage sexual activity, there is a growing body of evidence suggesting that such schemes may be proving counter-productive and are, in fact, leading to an increase in teenage sexual activity. They are also exposing young people to increased risk of sexual exploitation.

In Oxfordshire, for example, 'confidentiality was put before protection'.[33] In Hampshire, the parents of a vulnerable young teenager with special needs and sexual and emotional vulnerabilities were kept in the dark by professionals who took the view that her sexual activity and use of contraceptives was 'a confidential medical matter'.[34] The serious case review noted that '"Confidentiality" was used inappropriately to excuse failures to act.'[35]

The review team in Bristol similarly found that: 'The confusion created by national guidance on patient confidentiality, data protection and legal rights appears to get in the way of keeping child safeguarding as the

30 *Ibid.*

31 Sourafel Girma and David Paton, 'The Impact of Emergency Birth Control on Teen Pregnancy and STIs', *Journal of Health Economics*, 30(2), 2011, pp373-380.

32 Kasey S Buckles and Daniel M Hungerman, 'The incidental fertility effects of school condom distribution programs', *NBER Working Paper* 22322, June 2016.

33 Bedford, *Serious Case Review*, op. cit., para 8.52.

34 Harrington and Whyte, *The safeguarding implications*, op. cit., para 4.2.6.

35 *Ibid.*, para 6.1.15. At para 8.5, the report notes that 'confusion about confidentiality' was 'a consideration which was used inappropriately to excuse failures to take essential action'.

most paramount consideration.'[36] One of the teenage victims of sexual exploitation in Bristol issued the following plea:

> We want professionals, including sexual health nurses and GPs to ask us better questions, be more inquisitive and if necessary to examine us when we ask for morning after pills, or seem very young for contraception... Don't get so hung up on confidentiality, sometimes you do need to share what we have said.[37]

36 Myers and Carmi, *The Brooke Serious Case Review*, op. cit., para 8.1.9.

37 *Ibid.*, para 4.2.

CHAPTER 12
Guidance to GPs

'You can be sure that anything you discuss with any member of this practice - family doctor, nurse or receptionist - will stay confidential.

'Even if you are under 16 nothing will be said to anyone – including parents, other family members, care workers or tutors - without your permission.

The only reason why we might have to consider passing on confidential information without your permission, would be to protect you or someone else from serious harm. We would always try to discuss this with you first.'[1]

In line with Department of Health policies considered in the previous chapter, General Medical Council (GMC) guidance instructs doctors to respect the right of children to confidential consultations and to respect the decisions they make about the treatment they receive. The guidance states:

> You should make it clear that you are available to see children and young people on their own if that is what they want. You should avoid giving the impression (whether directly, through reception staff or in any other way) that they cannot access services without a parent. You should think carefully about the effect the presence of a chaperone can have. Their presence can deter young people from being frank and from asking for help.[2]

While the guidance insists that doctors must 'consider parents and others close to them'[3] and recognises that 'parents are usually the best judges of their children's best interests', it is equally insistent that doctors have 'the same duty of confidentiality to children and young people as [they] have to adults'.[4]

1 Example of a practice confidentiality statement, Royal College of General Practitioners, *Confidentiality and Young People Toolkit: Improving teenagers' uptake of sexual and other health advice*, 2011, p.57.

2 General Medical Council, *0-18 Years: Guidance for all doctors*, September 2007, para 15.

3 *Ibid.*, para 4.

4 *Ibid.*, para 21.

Conflict with child protection

The document acknowledges that there can be a conflict between child protection and confidentiality, but doctors are advised that children and young people should be entitled to confidential contraception, abortion and sexually transmitted infection advice and treatment provided they are judged to have the necessary maturity and ability to understand what is involved. This certainly applies to children as young as 13, and the guidance even falls short of advocating mandatory reporting below that age.

Doctors are advised that: 'You should *usually* share information about sexual activity involving children under 13, who are considered in law to be unable to consent.'[5] However, since the guidance takes the view that 'the capacity to consent depends more on young people's ability to understand and weigh up options than on age',[6] it leaves the door open to extending the right of confidentiality to sexually active pre-teens.

The word 'usually' appears again in connection with reporting 'abusive or seriously harmful sexual activity involving any child or young person'. Even in cases where the young person is too immature to understand or consent, where force, emotional or psychological pressure, bribery or payment is involved, where the young person's sexual partner has a position of trust, or where he or she is known to the police or child protection agencies as having had abusive relationships with children or young people, the GMC guidance falls short of advocating mandatory reporting.[7]

Purpose of guidance

The stated purpose of the guidance is 'to help doctors balance competing interests and make decisions that are ethical, lawful and for the good of children and young people'.[8] However, the GMC's commitment to ethics and lawfulness does not appear to extend to upholding the law on the age of consent to sexual intercourse.

The guidance asserts that, subject to the Fraser criteria, doctors can 'provide contraceptive, abortion and STI advice and treatment, without

5 *Ibid.*, para 67 (emphasis added).
6 *Ibid.*, para 25.
7 *Ibid.*, para 68.
8 *Ibid.*, para 9.

parental knowledge or consent, to young people under 16',[9] and claims that, 'A confidential sexual health service is essential for the welfare of children and young people'.[10] At no point does it consider the possibility that the provision of such confidential services might be jeopardising the welfare of children and young people by encouraging them to engage in sexual activity when they might not otherwise have done so.

The British Medical Association's (BMA) Children and young people ethics tool kit similarly advises doctors that their duty of confidentiality to a sexually active patient under the age of 16 takes precedence over the primary responsibility of the parent for the care of the child and over the law on the age of consent. The toolkit states:

> As with other medical interventions, a competent young person may give valid consent to abortion, contraception and treatment for a sexually transmitted infection, regardless of age or parental involvement, although every reasonable effort must be made to persuade the child to involve their parents or guardians.
>
> The courts have also confirmed that a parent's refusal to give consent for an abortion cannot override the consent of a competent young person.[11]

In response to the question, 'Does a doctor need to inform the police or social services of all underage sexual activity?' the BMA answers in the negative: 'No, only when there are concerns that the young person is being abused.' It then proceeds to refer to the GMC's 0-18 years guidance and adds:

> While reporting to social services or the police should always be considered where the individual is very young, the obligation of health professionals is to act in the best interests of the patient and this requires flexibility.[12]

The toolkit insists that in most cases the doctor does not need to inform the parents of a young person who is sexually active:

> If children under 16 are competent to understand what is involved in the proposed treatment, the health professional should, unless there are convincing reasons to the contrary, for instance abuse is suspected, respect the patient's wishes if they do not want their parents or guardians to know...

---

9 *Ibid.*, para 70.

10 *Ibid.*, para 64.

11 British Medical Association, *Children and young people ethics tool kit*, Chapter 10, 'Sexual Activity', 2016.

12 *Ibid.*

> An explicit request by a patient that information should not be disclosed to parents or guardians, or indeed to any third party must be respected save in the most exceptional circumstances, for example where the health, safety or welfare of the patient or another individual would be at risk.[13]

The current guidance to doctors and other medical practitioners is inhibiting professional curiosity and action.

The document goes on to state that, 'even where the health professional considers that a child is too immature to consent to the treatment requested' and does not grant it to them, 'confidentiality should still be respected concerning the consultation, unless there are very convincing reasons to the contrary'.[14]

While doctors have a right to exercise a conscientious objection to the provision of contraception or emergency hormonal birth control, the BMA toolkit insists that arrangements must be made for the child or young person to see another doctor as soon as possible.

The serious case reviews considered earlier in this report provide evidence that the current guidance to doctors and other medical practitioners is inhibiting 'professional curiosity and action'.[15] Even though Child D was only 13 when she conceived, the Liverpool serious case review reveals that the GP confirming the pregnancy did not enquire about the identity of the father or raise any concerns about her underage sexual activity.[16] In Thurrock, Julia had no difficulty in obtaining contraception from her GP,[17] and in Bristol, GPs took a similarly relaxed approach to sexual activity involving girls under the age of consent and prescribed contraception without expressing any concerns or sharing information.[18] The Bristol serious case review includes an example of a GP prescribing contraception for a girl of 13 who was believed to be in a consensual relationship with a 14 year-old boy, when in reality she was being exploited by an 18 year-old.[19]

The serious case reviews raise major questions about the common

13 *Ibid.*
14 *Ibid.*
15 Bedford, *Serious Case Review*, op. cit., paras 5.62, 5.63, 5.65, 5.146, 8.5, 9.6.
16 Liverpool Safeguarding Children Board, *Overview Report*, op. cit., para 3.3.3.
17 Wiffen and Peplow, *Serious Case Review*, op. cit.
18 Myers and Carmi, *The Brooke Serious Case Review*, op. cit., para 6.3.5.
19 *Ibid.*, para 6.3.6.

presumption that confidentiality policies are serving the best interests of children and young people. One victim from Bristol expressed amazement at the ease with which she was able to obtain the morning-after pill from her GP at the age of 13. The serious case review records:

> She said that at the time she wanted to say something more about what was happening but felt everything she said was taken at face value, on another occasion she says she had bruises and scratches on her thighs (she had been raped) but was never examined, again she wanted someone to be more curious.[20]

20 *Ibid.*, para 7.7.17.

CHAPTER 13
Guidance to school nurses

'School nurses are ideally placed for providing sexual health and contraceptive advice because of their relationship with young people: they are able to assess, supply emergency contraception, condoms, chlamydia screening, provide appropriate onward referral to sexual health services, and ensure follow-up with young people.'[1]

In the same way as GPs are instructed to offer a confidential service to children and young people, even where they are engaging in unlawful sexual activity, so guidance to school nurses places a strong emphasis on confidentiality. The Department for Education guidance on sex and relationships education draws a distinction between the role of a health professional delivering a sex education lesson on the one hand, and serving in a professional capacity on the other:

> Health professionals who are involved in delivering programmes are expected to work within the school's sex and relationship education policy and on the instructions of the head teacher. However, when they are in their professional role, such as a school nurse in a consultation with an individual pupil, they should follow their own professional codes of conduct (this is the case irrespective of who is paying them).[2]

Outside a teaching context, health professionals such as school nurses can:

- give one-to-one advice or information to a pupil on a health-related matter including contraception; and
- exercise their own professional judgment as to whether a young person has the maturity to consent to medical treatment including contraceptive treatment. (The criteria for making such a decision are based on the 'Fraser guidelines' and

1 Royal College of Nursing, *The role of school nurses in providing emergency contraception services in education settings*, RCN position statement, March 2012.

2 Department for Education and Employment, *Sex and Relationship Education Guidance*, Circular 0116/2000, July 2000, para 6.4.

can be found in guidance issued jointly by the Health Education Authority, the British Medical Association, Brook Advisory Centres and others. Any competent young person, regardless of age, can independently seek medical advice and give valid consent to treatment).[3]

School nurses and parents

For a number of years, the provision of contraceptive drugs in schools without parental knowledge or consent has been at variance with the government's 'good practice guide' with regard to the supply of medical treatment to pupils. The 1996 good practice guide on Supporting Pupils with Medical Needs unambiguously stated that there should be 'prior written agreement from parents or guardians for any medication, prescribed or non-prescription, to be given to a child' and that:

> School staff should generally not give non-prescribed medication to pupils [e.g. aspirin and paracetamol]. They may not know whether the pupil has taken a previous dose, or whether the medication may react with other medication being taken. **A child under 12 should never be given aspirin, unless prescribed** by a doctor . . . No pupil under the age of 16 should be given medication without his or her parent's written consent.[4]

However, school nurses employed by the health authority rather than by the school were not bound by education legislation and guidance, thus providing a mechanism to circumvent the government's 'good practice guide'. It was on this basis that the contraceptive pill and emergency hormonal birth control were made available to pupils without the knowledge or consent of their parents.

The 1996 guidance was superseded in 2005 by a document entitled *Managing Medicines in Schools and Early Years Settings*. The revised guidance continued to stress 'the need for prior written agreement from parents for any medicines to be given to a child' and insisted that 'No child under 16 should be given medicines without their parent's written consent.'[5]

A decade on, the guidance was updated once again. While it does

3 *Ibid.*, para 7.16.

4 Department for Education & Employment, Department of Health. *Supporting Pupils with Medical Needs: A good practice guide*. London: HMSO 1996 (emphasis in original).

5 Department for Education and Skills, Department of Health, *Managing Medicines in Schools and Early Years Settings*, Reference: 1448-2005DCL-EN, March 2005, paras 23, 42.

not make any explicit reference to contraception, there is a reference to medicine being given to pupils without parental consent in 'exceptional circumstances', out of respect to the child's 'right to confidentiality'. The current guidance insists that school policies should reflect the following practice:

> [N]o child under 16 should be given prescription or non-prescription medicines without their parent's written consent – except in exceptional circumstances where the medicine has been prescribed to the child without the knowledge of the parents. In such cases, every effort should be made to encourage the child or young person to involve their parents while respecting their right to confidentiality. Schools should set out the circumstances in which non-prescription medicines may be administered.[6]

The guidance in relation to contraception continues to stand in contrast to the administration of medication for pain relief. The Department for Education guidance goes on to state that:

> [A] child under 16 should never be given medicine containing aspirin unless prescribed by a doctor. Medication, e.g. for pain relief, should never be administered without first checking maximum dosages and when the previous dose was taken. Parents should be informed.[7]

Yet in spite of the fact that both aspirin and hormonal contraceptives can have serious, albeit rare, side-effects, contraception can be prescribed without parental involvement.

The school nurse as 'trusted confidante'

In 2006, the government issued fresh guidance for headteachers, teachers, support staff and governors to help them expand or develop a school nursing service that includes the provision of confidential contraceptive and abortion advice to underage pupils.

According to the document, *Looking for a School Nurse?* the provision of contraceptive advice, together with 'emergency contraception' and pregnancy testing on school premises, was intended to prevent teenage pregnancies and reduce the rates of sexually transmitted infections. The

---

6 Department for Education, *Supporting pupils at school with medical conditions: Statutory guidance for governing bodies of maintained schools and proprietors of academies in England*, December 2015, p.20.

7 *Ibid.*

guidance stated that one of the 'advanced functions' of the school nurse will be to act as a 'trusted confidante', able to 'offer support and advice to young people concerned with issues of sexual identity'.[8]

The *School Nurse Practice Development Resource Pack* was published at the same time with a view to offering best practice guidance to school nurses and public health officials. According to the resource pack, 'school nurses can raise sexual health and relationship issues with young people and make sure they have access to the kind of information and services they need'. As part of 'best practice', school nurses were encouraged to:

- Provide and promote confidential drop-ins at school and community venues ensuring they are linked to wider primary health care, family planning and genito-urinary medicine (GUM) services. Consider the use of new technologies such as texting or e-mail to improve access...
- Support young women to access services to make timely choices about emergency contraception, pregnancy or abortion…
- Clarify the purpose and boundary of your role within SRE [sex and relationships education], ensure it is clear to young people, use ground rules in sessions and remind young people where they can access confidential support and information.[9]

A document published with the express aim of helping school nurses to tackle child sexual exploitation reiterates the importance of a confidential school-based nursing service. Jointly published by the Department of Health and Public Health England, the guidance states that:

> **School nursing teams have a role in raising awareness and supporting children at risk of sexual exploitation, and must:**
> Provide an accessible, confidential school nursing service that is conducive to building rapport and trust between practitioner and children and young people…
>
> and
>
> **School nursing teams must ensure their services are young people friendly by:…**

8 Department for Education and Skills, Department of Health, *Looking for a school nurse?* 2006, p.17.
9 Department for Education and Skills, Department of Health, *School Nurse: Practice Development Resource Pack*, 2006, pp.23-24.

> Developing accessible, reliable services in schools that are friendly and offer a confidential, non-judgemental service.[10]

There is no reference in the document to respecting the age of consent, nor to the need to promote a culture that discourages underage sex. The Brook Sexual Behaviours Traffic Light Tool is signposted as a resource.[11]

The various guidance documents for school nurses are inevitably having the effect of normalising unlawful sex under the age of 16 and thus exposing children and young people to increased risk of sexual exploitation and abuse.

10 Department of Health and Public Health England, *Helping school nurses to tackle child sexual exploitation*, 2015.

11 See chapter 17.

CHAPTER 14

Sex education and the reluctance to consider anything 'wrong'

[T]here was...an acceptance of a degree of underage sexual activity that reflects a wider societal reluctance to consider something 'wrong'.[1]

It is frequently claimed that sex and relationships education (SRE) has a key role to play in addressing child sexual exploitation and keeping children and young people safe.[2] Many children's charities and campaigning organisations have been pressing for some time to make PSHE (Personal, Social, Health and Economic education), including SRE, a statutory part of the curriculum for both primary and secondary school pupils. Vera Baird, the Northumbria Police and Crime Commissioner went so far as to say that compulsory PSHE is 'the one step that can protect young people'.[3]

The campaign for statutory PSHE/SRE also has the support of a number of parliamentary committees and several inquiries have recommended changing the status of the subject area. For example, the Stockport MP, Ann Coffey, was commissioned by the Police and Crime Commissioner for Greater Manchester to conduct an independent inquiry into the work that has been undertaken to tackle child sexual exploitation in the area since the Rochdale serious case review had been published. Her report called for a campaign 'to make PSHE compulsory so that all children in Greater Manchester schools are better safeguarded from CSE', though in this instance the report did concede that compulsory PSHE 'would not in itself guarantee the quality of the information taught'.[4]

---

1 Bedford, *Serious Case Review*, op. cit., para 5.23.

2 See, for example, Sex Education Forum, *Addressing healthy sexual relationships and sexual exploitation within PSHE in schools*, Forum factsheet 37, October 2006.

3 Vera Baird, 'Sex education is the only way to combat the terrible toll of child abuse', *Guardian*, 1 August 2016.

4 Ann Coffey MP, *Real Voices: Child sexual exploitation in Greater Manchester*, October 2014, pp. 43, 78, 81.

Rather than make PSHE or SRE a statutory part of the national curriculum, others have proposed the creation of a new curriculum subject to be known as Relationship Education. In a report published in 2014, the Centre for Social Justice (CSJ) recommended that Relationship Education should be made compulsory in its own right so that 'national standards could be applied and children could not be withdrawn from it'.[5]

Although the new subject would incorporate sex education, the CSJ was confident that statutory Relationship Education would not arouse the same degree of controversy as statutory SRE. It therefore declared: 'Our proposal avoids confronting any reluctance to make SRE compulsory due to sensitivities around mandating discussions in schools about young people's attitudes towards sex.'[6]

In an amendment to the Children and Social Work Bill in March 2017, the government adopted a modified version of the CSJ proposal, whereby Relationships Education will become a statutory subject in all primary schools, and all secondary schools will be required to teach Relationships and Sex Education. The move has been welcomed by the leading campaigners for statutory SRE, but what is it that they want all children to learn? And is there any evidence that it will keep them safe?

Relativism

The Sex Education Forum describes itself as 'the national authority on sex and relationships education' and includes among its more prominent members the PSHE Association, Brook, the *fpa* and the NSPCC. The Forum's commitment to relativism is reflected in its government-funded toolkit, *Are you getting it right?* The toolkit contains a series of activities designed to encourage pupils to share their views about what they want to learn in SRE, how they want to learn, and what support and advice they want and need. The activity on a 'moral and values framework' makes it clear that the purpose is 'not to agree the rights and wrongs' of various statements, 'but rather to discover the range of opinions on the subject'.[7]

An *fpa* leaflet for young people states it much more baldly: 'What's right for YOU is what's important.'[8] The position is explained more fully

5 Centre for Social Justice, *Fully Committed? How a Government could reverse family breakdown*, July 2014.

6 *Ibid.*, p.42.

7 Sex Education Forum, *Are you getting it right? A toolkit for consulting young people on sex and relationships education*, February 2008, p.23.

8 *fpa, Is everybody doing it? A guide to contraception*, 2014.

in another *fpa* publication:

> How do you know you love someone? When is it right to have sex? How do you know you are ready? When are you ready to have children? How can you be sure marriage is right for you or not? Should you only have one partner at a time? These questions that have been dilemmas over many generations are increased by the modern pressures on young people to be as adventurous and accumulative in their sexual lives as they are expected to be in their material lives. Few of us can offer simple answers to young people – yes or no, this is right or wrong. Our task is to assist the young to find their way through life's minefields as confidently, positively and unharmed as possible.[9]

This relativistic approach has also found its way into guidance offered to parents to assist them in speaking to their children about sensitive issues. According to a leaflet approved by government ministers, parents should not teach their children that there are any rights and wrongs when it comes to sex and relationships. The leaflet, *Talking to your teenager about sex and relationships*, tells parents that their children need to know about contraception, sexually transmitted infections, gay, lesbian and bi-sexual teenagers, and alcohol and drugs, but warns parents that teaching their children that anything is right or wrong will be counterproductive. While parents may discuss their 'values' with their teenage children, they are urged to:

> Remember though, that trying to convince them of what's right and wrong may discourage them from being open. Try to keep the discussion light, encourage them to say what they think and reassure them that you trust them to make the right decisions.[10]

There are several references to 'right decisions' and 'right choices', but they are only ever defined in connection with using contraception – what the leaflet inaccurately describes as 'safe sex'. The message communicated is that there is nothing wrong about any kind of sexual relationship in principle, so long as contraception is used.

In 2014, the PSHE Association, the Sex Education Forum and Brook published 'supplementary advice' to be used alongside the

---

9 Doreen E Massey (ed), *Sex Education Source Book: Current issues and debates, fpa*, 1995, p.44.

10 NHS, *Talking to your teenager about sex and relationships*, 2009.

Department for Education Sex and Relationship Education guidance.[11] However, at several points, the tone and content of the advice is not so much 'supplementary' as contradictory. For example, Section 403 of the Education Act 1996 stipulates that sex education must be given in such a manner that it encourages pupils to have 'due regard to moral considerations and the value of family life'. It goes on to insist that formal guidance must ensure that sex education teaches 'the nature of marriage and its importance for family life and the bringing up of children'.

However, the advice produced by Brook, the Sex Education Forum and the PSHE Association is devoid of references to morality, marriage or family life. While it talks about treating sex as 'a normal and pleasurable fact of life', it has nothing to say about the moral context in which sex is to be enjoyed. There is not even a reference to the need for fidelity and exclusivity. It is as though such considerations are completely irrelevant to sex education. The advice asserts that 'SRE is part of the solution to concerns about sexualisation', but fails to recognise that it can also be part of the problem when it is presented outside a clear and firm moral framework.

More recent guidance from the PSHE Association places a strong emphasis on 'non-judgmental classroom discussion', which is described as 'a key feature of high-quality PSHE education'. In a joint foreword, then Home Secretary, Theresa May, and then Education Secretary, Nicky Morgan, welcomed the guidance as 'an excellent resource which will help [teachers] provide pupils with the skills and knowledge to keep themselves and others informed, healthy and safe'.[12]

In the name of non-judgmentalism, the approach advocated by the leading SRE campaigners, and endorsed by the government, is abandoning young people to the shifting sands of relativism and depriving them of the moral compass they desperately need. As a former US Secretary of Education noted:

> [Y]ou sometimes get the feeling that, for these guides, being 'comfortable' with one's decision when exercising one's 'option' is the sum and substance of the responsible life. Decisions aren't right or wrong – decisions simply make you comfortable or not. It is as though 'comfort' alone had now become our moral compass.[13]

11 Brook, PSHE Association, Sex Education Forum, *Sex and Relationships Education (SRE) for the 21st Century*, 2014. *http://www.sexeducationforum.org.uk/media/17706/sreadvice.pdf*

12 PSHE Association, *Teaching about consent in PSHE Education at key stages 3 and 4*, March 2015.

13 William Bennett, 'Sex and the Education of our Children', an address delivered at a meeting of the National

'Inappropriate' teaching

It promoted sex as a wonderful feeling and exciting - no wonder some of the children now wanted to try it!

In spite of the fact that education law aims to protect children from 'inappropriate' teaching and materials,[14] large numbers of children are being introduced to sexual themes at school in an inappropriate way and at an inappropriate stage in their development.

For example, several parents have reported instances where primary school pupils have simulated sex after viewing cartoon depictions of intercourse in the Channel 4 resource, *Living and Growing*, which is commended by the Sex Education Forum and used widely in primary school sex education lessons. One parent wrote:

> [T]he effects of what our children had been taught [soon] became alarmingly apparent. Children were found simulating sex on top of other children and some children were telling much younger children what they had learned, much to the horror of their parents. Still others were openly stating to parents that they now wanted to have sex.
>
> Some children, including my daughter, became very upset and worried about the whole matter. She was not emotionally or mentally able to cope with this information...
>
> I [finally] managed to find out what DVD the school had used and I and other parents watched it on the Internet in horror. It was so graphic and the narrative was appalling. It promoted sex as a wonderful feeling and exciting - no wonder some of the children now wanted to try it![15]

Teaching pornography

Recent years have seen mounting calls for pornography to feature prominently in sex education lessons, amid growing concerns about its ready availability online and evidence that it is being accessed by large

School Boards Association in January 1987.

14 Section 403 of the Education Act 1996 places the Secretary of State under an obligation to issue guidance designed to ensure that when sex education is given to registered pupils at maintained schools, '...they are protected from teaching and materials which are inappropriate having regard to the age and the religious and cultural background of the pupils concerned'.

15 Lisa Bullivant, Family Education Trust *Bulletin*, Issue 140, Summer 2010.

numbers of children and young people. But here, too, a commitment to relativism and non-judgmentalism is leading to the introduction of teaching in schools that is exposing young people to sexually explicit materials and ideas.

Many people are inclined to support the campaign to teach pupils about pornography in schools on the assumption that the purpose of the lessons would be to discourage children and young people from accessing it. However, the reality is quite different.

Some advocates of pornography education use very sophisticated language to make it sound respectable. For example, Justin Hancock of Bish Training writes:

> Being able to talk about porn with kids gives an opportunity to talk about: self esteem, body image, sexual decision making, boundaries, pleasure, consent, orgasm, communication, safer sex, sexual safety, the law, feminism, equality, list *(sic)* and love, emotions, relationships, masculine norms, sex scripts, sexuality and oppression.

Yet, in the very next paragraph, he reveals that in practice the kind of pornography education he has in mind is much more graphic and explicit:

> Many people's sex education from parents is simply 'don't get anyone pregnant' or 'don't have sex till you're older'. Talking about porn is a great way to introduce big topics that young people want to talk about. Asking questions like 'why does the camera always seem to focus on the woman in straight porn' or 'why does sex end when the guy orgasms' or 'what do you think about the language used to describe people and sexual activity in porn' brings up areas that might not otherwise be discussed.[16]

The Sex Education Forum recommends 'Planet Porn', a pack of resources produced by Bish Training.[17] The pack includes a game comprised of 36 cards, each bearing a different statement. Pupils take it in turns to decide whether the statement belongs on 'Planet Earth' (real life sex) or 'Planet Porn' (porn sex). Each statement has an accompanying card which provides additional information and further points for discussion.

Other activities in the pack include 'Porn Challenge', which is

16 Justin Hancock, 'What to do if you find your kid is watching porn', bishuk.com.

17 Sex Education Forum, *The Sex Education Supplement*, Vol 1, Issue 1, April 2013.

designed to help young people 'to think of ways to present sexy scenes and images which are safe, promote equality and diversity and don't make assumptions about who may be watching porn'. Then there is 'Dear Doctor Love', described as 'a problem page activity which explores relationship issues like trust, intimacy, boundaries, safety, jealousy, independence, self-esteem and communication through the medium of problems that a partner of a pornstar or sexy model might face'.[18]

The Sex Education Forum also recommends a page on *TheSite* website entitled 'Porn vs Reality',[19] which advises young people: 'Sex is great. And porn can be great. It's the idea that porn sex is like real sex which is the problem. But if you can separate the fantasy from the reality you're much more likely to enjoy both.'[20]

The Sex Education Forum's e-magazine on pornography includes a 'Teachers' wishlist' which states: 'We want teachers to know... That pornography is hugely diverse – it's not necessarily "all bad".'[21]

In a similar vein, Bish Training's 'Planet Porn' includes a 'Porn Debate' resource which, the publishers state, 'tries to be even handed and doesn't attempt to tell people whether porn is good or bad. This activity gives young people the chance to think about and to build on their own values around various ethical questions in porn.'[22]

On his website for young people aged 14 and above, the creator of Bish Training, Justin Hancock, lists several distasteful scenarios involving teenagers accessing different kinds of pornography, but leaves it up to his young readers to decide for themselves whether they are right or wrong. 'Your call,' he writes, 'I'm not going to tell you what to think!'[23] As with the Sex Education Forum's e-magazine, the assumption is made that not all pornography is 'bad' and no moral guidance is given.

To help children to be sufficiently 'media literate' so that they can properly 'interpret' pornography and enjoy it more hardly seems a worthy educational goal. Many would question whether schools that provide such education merit being regarded 'safe spaces'. Such teaching would merely compound the problems associated with the sexualisation of children.

18 Bish Training website, 'Planet Porn'.

19 Sex Education Forum, *The Sex Education Supplement*, op. cit.

20 TheSite has now been rebranded as The Mix, but the feature on 'Porn vs Reality' remains. *http://www.themix.org.uk/sex-and/porn/porn-vs-reality-3917.html* Accessed 15 February 2017.

21 Sex Education Forum, *The Sex Education Supplement*, op. cit.

22 Bish Training website, *op. cit.*

23 Justin Hancock, 'Porn laws –is it legal, is it right?' bishuk.com, 6 September 2011.

For some pupils it would run the very real danger of arousing a curiosity to search out more pornography for themselves, and for others it might very well introduce the idea for the very first time.

In common with other members of the Sex Education Forum, the PSHE Association has long argued that teaching children about different sexual practices does not influence their behaviour and encourage sexual experimentation. However, on the issue of self-harm, the association has conceded that graphic depictions and descriptions of self-harming could serve as a 'trigger' to young people vulnerable to self-harm. In urging schools not to use the Channel 4 documentary 'My Self-Harm Nightmare' in class, the PSHE Association's Mental Health and Emotional Wellbeing Advisor, Dr Pooky Knightsmith, commented:

> You should never go into too much detail about the technical details of self-harm or eating disorders as this could trigger unhealthy responses in any vulnerable individuals in your group. Talking about specific methods of self-harm can be instructive to vulnerable students. These suggestions may also be taken on board by any students who are currently harming.[24]

It is difficult to see why these same arguments should not be applied equally to sex education lessons.

But does it work?

Campaigners for statutory PSHE/SRE claim that there is overwhelming evidence in support of their cause. In reality, however, the supporting evidence is in short supply and surprisingly little research has been conducted to evaluate the success of sex education programmes. An external steering group established by the last Labour government noted that:

> [T]here is a dearth of good quality international evidence on SRE. A literature review of the international evidence that does exist confirms that it is difficult to be precise about the impact of SRE, for a number of reasons. Firstly, there is not always clarity about what the objectives of SRE are... Second, there is such significant variation in the delivery of SRE that it makes comparisons between programmes difficult.'[25]

24 PSHE Association press release, 'PSHE Association warns against using Ch4 "My Self-Harm Nightmare" documentary in class', 23 March 2015.

25 *Review of Sex and Relationship Education (SRE) in Schools: A report by the External Steering Group*, October

An examination of one 'enhanced sex education programme', for example, found that while the programme increased young people's knowledge it had no discernable effect on sexual activity.[26] The lead researcher, Dr Marion Henderson commented, 'It may be that we have already seen the limits of what sex education can achieve and we need to look wider at parenting and the culture in which children grow up.'[27]

A review of evaluations of a number of sex education initiatives undertaken by Professor Lawrie Elliott from Edinburgh Napier University found that they had little or no positive impact on the sexual behaviour of young people. He concluded that we may have reached a threshold in what can be achieved by population based interventions and commented: 'Our findings challenge the conventional wisdom that traditional public health methods such as education in schools linked to sexual health clinics are able to affect the sexual health of the neediest in society.'[28]

A recent Cochrane review of the effects of school-based sexual and reproductive health programmes on sexually transmitted infections (such as HIV, herpes simplex virus, and syphilis), and pregnancy among adolescents found 'little evidence that educational curriculum-based programmes alone are effective in improving sexual and reproductive health outcomes for adolescents'.[29]

The trials included in the review evaluated educational programmes which incorporated many of the specific characteristics that have previously been recommended for 'well-designed adolescent sexual and reproductive health interventions'. However, they still 'failed to demonstrate any reduction in the prevalence of STIs or adolescent pregnancy'.

Keeping young people safe

But what about the claim that sex and relationships education holds

2008, para 22. See also T Stammers, 'Sexual health in adolescents: "Saved sex" and parental involvement are key to improving outcomes', *BMJ*, 2007, 334:103-4.

26 M Henderson, 'Impact of a theoretically based sex education programme (SHARE) delivered by teachers on NHS registered conceptions and terminations: final results of cluster randomised trial', *BMJ*, 2007, 334:133.

27 Celia Hall, 'Role-playing sex classes fail to cut abortions', *Daily Telegraph*, 21 November 2006.

28 Edinburgh Napier University press release, 14 September 2010.

29 A J Mason-Jones, D Sinclair, C Mathews, A Kagee, A Hillman, C Lombard, 'School-based interventions for preventing HIV, sexually transmitted infections, and pregnancy in adolescents'. Cochrane Database of Systematic Reviews 2016, Issue 11. Art. No.: CD006417. DOI: 10.1002/14651858.CD006417.pub3.

the key to keeping children and young people safe? This is an argument which has come more to the fore in recent months. Yet, the evidence from the serious case reviews suggests that the relativistic approach advocated by the leading campaigners for statutory sex education is not the solution, but is rather part of the problem.

'Action to prevent harm' should always take precedence over 'action to be non-judgmental'.

The Bristol serious case review notes 'an underlying confusion for practitioners in distinguishing between underage but consensual sexual activity between peers and child sexual abuse and sexual exploitation'.[30] But that confusion does not exist in a vacuum. It is rather 'rooted in the complex and contradictory cultural, legal and moral norms around sexuality, and in particular teenage sexual experimentation'.[31] Part of the problem lies in the moral confusion that has resulted from an abandonment of moral absolutes.

This theme is pursued further in the Oxfordshire report. Having made the observation that there were times when 'confidentiality was put before protection',[32] the report suggests that for at least some professionals this related to 'a reluctance to take a moral stance on right and wrong, and seeing being non-judgmental as the overriding principle'.[33] The Oxfordshire report further states that: '[T]here was…an acceptance of a degree of underage sexual activity that reflects a wider societal reluctance to consider something "wrong",'[34] and argues that 'action to prevent harm' should always take precedence over 'action to be non-judgmental'.[35]

In a most telling comment, the report notes that 'the reluctance in many places, both political and professional, to have any firm statements about something being "wrong"' is among the factors that create 'an environment where it is easier for vulnerable young people/children to be exploited. It also makes it harder for professionals to have the confidence and bravery to be more proactive on prevention and intervention.'[36]

30 Myers and Carmi, *The Brooke Serious Case Review*, op. cit., para 7.2.18.
31 *Ibid.*
32 Bedford, *Serious Case Review*, op. cit., para 8.52.
33 *Ibid.*, para 8.53.
34 *Ibid.*, para 5.23.
35 *Ibid.*, para 8.58.
36 *Ibid.*, para 8.55.

In the light of these observations from the serious case reviews, we should be wary any approach to sex and relationships education that is reluctant to declare anything 'wrong'. Children, young people and professionals alike all need a clear moral compass in order to safely negotiate the confused and confusing landscape that lies before them.

CHAPTER 15
Sex education: undermining parents and pursuing short-term goals

'In reducing sexual safety and responsibility to the use of a condom and the acquisition of consent, comprehensive sex education sends the inaccurate and dangerous message that these two precautions allow one to have lots of sex without consequences.

'[C]omprehensive sex education programmes…regularly disconnect sex from the context of a committed, loving, exclusive relationship (i.e. marriage). This saturates the young imagination and whets the appetite not for a relationship but for sex itself, disconnected from any person or commitment of love… Contemporary sex education prepares young men and women not for the fullness of friendship, intimacy and love, but for casual relationships and recreational sex…

'[C]omprehensive sex education programmes at the primary, secondary, and collegiate levels do young men and women a disservice by training them year after year in attitudes and behaviors that undercut their chances of future marital success.'[1]

In our analysis of the reports on child sexual exploitation in Part One, we noted that the tendency to disregard parental concerns and even to view parents as a nuisance was a recurring theme. For example:

- In Rotherham, fathers who traced their daughters and tried to rescue them from their abusers were themselves arrested.[2] The concerns of one Rotherham mother were dismissed on the basis that she was not able to accept that her daughter was growing up, when in reality, the

1 Cassandra Hough, 'Learning about Love: How Sex Ed Programs Undermine Happy Marriages', Witherspoon Institute, *Public Discourse*, 29 October 2014.

2 Jay, *Independent Inquiry*, op. cit., para 5.9.

young teenager was being sexually exploited.[3]

- The Oxfordshire report refers to 'distraught, desperate and terrified parents [who] were sometimes seen as part of the problem'.[4] The concerns of parents were ignored and not given the weight they deserved.
- In Hampshire, 'There was little evidence of alertness to the need to consider informing and involving parents' when Child F's underage sexual activity became apparent.[5]
- Similarly, in Bristol, professionals from key agencies 'did not listen enough to the concerns of parents' when they described the sexual exploitation their children were being subjected to.[6]

Sad to say, the leading campaigners for statutory sex and relationships education have encouraged an ambivalent attitude towards parents.

This is reflected in the 'supplementary advice' produced by the Sex Education Forum, Brook and the PSHE Association. Whereas the statutory government guidance contains over 90 references to parents and stresses the importance of consultation with parents and taking into account their wishes and concerns, the advice of the sex education lobby plays down the role of parents.

Although the advice maintains that 'high quality SRE' is 'a partnership between home and school', it places more emphasis on actively seeking the views of children and young people to influence lesson planning and teaching than it does on consultation with parents. In fact, it chooses to state that 'Parents and carers *can* be invited to see the resources that the school has selected',[7] rather than take the more positive line that schools 'should' invite parents to review their sex education resources.

Undermining parents

The exaltation of the desires of the child at the expense of the wishes of the parent is finding its way into some sex and relationships education policies. For example, the Elliot Foundation, which runs a chain of primary academies states in its policy that: 'children's views and attitudes

3 *Ibid.*, para 3.23.

4 Bedford, *Serious Case Review*, op. cit., para 8.5 and Appendix 1.

5 Harrington and Whyte, *The safeguarding implications*, op. cit., para 6.1.17.

6 Myers and Carmi, *The Brooke Serious Case Review*, op. cit., para 6.3.1.

7 Brook, PSHE Association, Sex Education Forum, *Sex and Relationships Education (SRE) for the 21st Century*, op. cit., p.13, (emphasis added).

should be assessed through the academy's "pupil voice" processes e.g. via the School Council'. However, there is no reference to any corresponding mechanism to ascertain the views of parents. The nearest the foundation's policy comes to mentioning any form of consultation with parents is when it states that the principal shall ensure that 'a consultative partnership is developed with parents to ensure that there is a clear understanding of the policy and to address any concerns they may have'.[8] In reality, however, this 'consultative partnership' amounts to little more than the sharing of information. It is a far cry from the type of engagement required in the statutory guidance.

The idea that children and young people should have an influence in determining the character of the sex education they receive sounds very democratic and may look very reasonable at first glance, but there is a subtle undermining of parental responsibility lurking just below the surface. It is parents who are responsible in law for ensuring that their children receive an efficient full-time education suitable to their age, ability and aptitude,[9] and education law upholds the principle that pupils are to be educated according to the wishes of their parents.[10]

In the spheres of health, education and child protection, it is to be feared that children are increasingly being treated as autonomous individuals divorced from the supervision of their parents.

'When you are ready'

Having consciously abandoned moral absolutes in favour of a firm commitment to relativism and undermined parents, the leading sex education campaigners have turned their attention to helping children and young people to have safe and fulfilling sexual relationships 'when they are ready'.[11] There is little, if any, emphasis on preparation for the lifelong marriage that most young people aspire to.

Yet many of the victims of sexual exploitation described in the first part of this report believed that they were 'ready' for a sexual relationship and that their abusers were their 'boyfriends'. The Independent Inquiry

8 The Elliot Foundation, Sex and Relationships Education policy, June 2016.

9 Education Act 1996, s7.

10 Education Act 1996, s9.

11 For example, in its position statement on child sexual exploitation, Brook states: 'Brook believes that children and young people deserve healthy, consensual relationships when they are ready and able to take responsibility for them and that CSE breaches those rights.' *https://www.brook.org.uk/about-brook/brook-position-statement-child-sexual-exploitation-cse*

into Child Sexual Exploitation in Rotherham found that:

> *A common feature of child sexual exploitation is that the child or young person does not recognise the coercive nature of the relationship and does not see himself or herself as a victim of exploitation.*

A common feature of child sexual exploitation is that the child or young person does not recognise the coercive nature of the relationship and does not see himself or herself as a victim of exploitation.

> Typically, children were courted by a young man whom they believed to be their boyfriend. Over a period of time, the child would be introduced to older men who cultivated them and supplied them with gifts, free alcohol and sometimes drugs. Children were initially flattered by the attention paid to them, and impressed by the apparent wealth and sophistication of those grooming them…
>
> Many were utterly convinced that they were special in the affections of a perpetrator, despite all the evidence that many other children were being groomed and abused by the same person.[12]

The Oxfordshire serious case review cites the minutes of a meeting of the Prostitution Strategy Youth Group which reported that:

> anecdotal evidence had come to light of young girls who were being groomed by much older men in Oxford. The men were buying expensive gifts for the girls who believed them to be their 'boyfriend'.[13]

The report refers to a 14 year-old girl who was taking cannabis daily, taking cocaine at parties and drinking up to 45 units of alcohol in a single night; she also referred to a 19 year-old 'boyfriend'.[14] As the report later notes, 'The benign word "boyfriend" disguised age-inappropriate relationships.'[15]

The Bristol serious case review observes that:

> A common feature of CSE is that the child or young person does not recognise the coercive nature of the relationship and does not see himself or herself as a victim of exploitation.[16]

The report goes on to note that, among other things, child sexual

12 Jay, *Independent Inquiry*, op. cit., paras 5.17-18.
13 Bedford, *Serious Case Review, op. cit.*, para 7.36.
14 *Ibid.*, para 5.144.
15 *Ibid.*, para 8.53.
16 Myers and Carmi, *The Brooke Serious Case Review*, op. cit., para 2.4.1.

exploitation can refer to:

- Inappropriate, sexually exploitative relationships where the young person believes the abuser to be their boyfriend or girlfriend, perceiving him/herself to be in a romantic relationship with this individual, and
- Groups of adults abusing children, often through a particular adult seen as a 'boyfriend' by the victim of the abuse.[17]

Children and those around them frequently have difficulty in identifying sexual exploitation because the abusers identify themselves as 'boyfriends'. Barnardo's describe it as a 'boyfriend model of exploitation and peer exploitation'.[18] Mandating the inclusion of teaching about consent in SRE would therefore not solve the problem. Due weight needs to be given to other moral considerations above and beyond the matter of consent.

The message that children and young people must be left free to decide for themselves 'when they are ready' to embark on a sexual relationship is failing them and exposing them to the risk of sexual exploitation. So, too, is the idea that sexual expression is a means to self-gratification and enjoyment.

The quest for sexual pleasure

Recent years have seen a growing emphasis on sexual pleasure in sex and relationships education. In the words of Gill Frances, who has served as co-ordinator of the Sex Education Forum and as chair of the government's Teenage Pregnancy Independent Advisory Group (TPIAG), 'discussions on sexual pleasure help children realise sex should be enjoyed, allowing them to take responsibility for decisions and recognise issues around coercive sex'.[19]

A 16-page booklet produced by the Centre for HIV and Sexual Health at NHS Sheffield entitled *Pleasure* advises health workers on 'why and how to raise the issue of sexual pleasure in sexual health work with young people'.[20] Written by Steve Slack, the Centre's director and a member of Independent Advisory Group for Sexual Health, with input

17 *Ibid.*

18 *Ibid.*, para 7.2.16.

19 *Children & Young People Now*, 24 September 2009.

20 Centre for HIV and Sexual Health, *Pleasure: A Booklet for Workers on Why and How to Raise the Issue of Sexual Pleasure in Sexual Health Work with Young People*, NHS Sheffield.

from TPIAG member Professor Roger Ingham, the booklet warns: 'Young people will be adults in intimate relationships in the future. If they don't have knowledge about giving and receiving sexual pleasure, their relationships could suffer.' The publication goes on to stress: 'A key message to convey is that everyone engaged in consenting sexual activity has a right to fun, enjoyment and fulfilment or, in other words, to sexual pleasure.'[21] According to Dr Slack:

> Sex education, which includes information about sexual pleasure, is not about promoting sexual activity. It is about promoting the sexual rights of all individuals. Everyone needs accurate information and skills to make informed choices and to negotiate the type of sex which is good and pleasurable for them.[22]

The idea of sexual intimacy having anything to do with commitment and self-giving is totally absent from the booklet, and love receives only passing mention. The whole focus is on the short-lived pleasure to be derived from fleeting sexual encounters, rather than on preparing young people for the lasting pleasures of a lifelong union based on something deeper than physical attraction and self-gratification.

It is highly doubtful, however, whether it is realistic to combine information about sexual pleasure with the message that 'everyone' has a 'right' to it and then not expect young people to want to try it. It is a message that is playing into the hands of the unscrupulous, who stand ready to exploit it to their own ends.

The message conveyed by the *Pleasure* booklet is: 'Sex is fun, it's fulfilling, you have a right to it, you deserve it, you can have it when you want and how you want; it's yours for the asking.' It is difficult to imagine a way more calculated to promote sexual experimentation and encourage self-indulgence.

A similar emphasis on sexual pleasure is found on the *Respect Yourself* website.[23] The site has been designed for children and young people from the age of 13 with the stated aim of encouraging them to access sexual health services, but the campaign team recognises that even younger children will access the site and states that 'some of the information may be useful for young people experiencing puberty'.[24] But that does

21 *Ibid.*, p.3.
22 *Ibid.*, p.7.
23 Warwickshire County Council, op. cit., *https://respectyourself.info/* Accessed 16 February 2017.
24 'Let's talk about sex', *Warwickshire News*, 10 October 2012.

not inhibit the site's creators from encouraging sexual experimentation. Young visitors to the site are advised:

> There are many different ways that two people can fit together and have sex with each other. Everybody is different, there are no right or wrong ways to 'do it' – the fun is experimenting and exploring with your partner(s).[25]

The site employs crude and even foul language, features sexual practices that it acknowledges are 'perversions', and treats the age of consent with contempt. Not only does it include explicit photographs of both male and female genitals and highlight erogenous zones, but it includes 'flirting tips' and a 'sextionary', consisting of an A-Z of 'medical, technical, slang and downright weird and full words to do with sex, your body and relationships'.

In response to concerns expressed about the *Respect Yourself* website, the then Health Minister Anna Soubry stated:

> It is important to ensure that young people have access to information about relationships and sexual health in a format that is easy to access, and that uses language and methods of communication that they feel are aimed at them. As I have mentioned, I do not consider the content of the website to be troubling.[26]

The website was shortlisted for the Brook Sexual Health Awards in 2014,[27] and its creators have a vision for seeing it replicated elsewhere. *Respect Yourself* Campaign Manager, Amy Danahay, commented: 'This is the first website of its kind in the country and we hope to be pioneers for other authorities.'[28]

'Comprehensive sex and relationships education'

The 'supplementary advice' on sex education produced by the Sex Education Forum, the PSHE Association and Brook makes several references to 'comprehensive sex and relationships education' programmes. The term 'comprehensive' sounds reassuring. After all, do we not want education to be thorough rather than piecemeal? But the term 'comprehensive sexuality education' has a particular meaning to sex educators which is

---

25 Warwickshire County Council, *op. cit.*, 'Positions', *http://respectyourself.info/sextionary/#positions* Accessed 16 February 2017.

26 Letter from Anna Soubry to Family Education Trust, 4 February 2013.

27 Better2Know, 'UK Sexual Health Awards 2014'.

28 'Let's talk about sex', *op. cit.*

imbued with the spirit of relativism and focussed on the here and now rather than on the future lives of children and young people.

With its emphasis on sexual pleasure divorced from the context of a lifelong loving union, comprehensive sex education creates in young people the expectation that they will have a series of casual sexual relationships.

UNESCO defines comprehensive sexuality education as:

> an age-appropriate, culturally relevant approach to teaching about sex and relationships by providing scientifically accurate, realistic, non-judgmental information. Sexuality education provides opportunities to explore one's own values and attitudes and to build decision-making, communication and risk reduction skills about many aspects of sexuality. The term comprehensive emphasizes an approach to sexuality education that encompasses the full range of information, skills and values to enable young people to exercise their sexual and reproductive rights and to make decisions about their health and sexuality.[29]

The focus is on the sexual pleasure of young people in the present, combined with reducing the risk of conception and sexually transmitted infections rather than seeking to prepare them for a lifelong faithful marriage.

In an insightful article, the social commentator Cassandra Hough observes that comprehensive sex education 'may purport to aim at sexual risk reduction, but it effectively instructs young men and women in sexual risk-taking'. She continues:

> It sets up abstinence as an unrealistic ideal and neglects adequate discussion of the importance of sexual restraint and the attitudes, behaviours, and environments that best enable young people to practice that restraint. It encourages condom use as a means of reducing risk while simultaneously normalising behaviours that make the incidence of sex more frequent and that create environments of increased vulnerability. In reducing sexual safety and responsibility to the use of a condom and the acquisition of consent, comprehensive sex education sends the inaccurate and dangerous message that these two precautions allow one to have

29 UNESCO, 'Sexuality Education'. *http://www.unesco.org/new/en/hiv-and-aids/our-priorities-in-hiv/sexuality-education/* Accessed 16 February 2017.

lots of sex without consequences.[30]

With its emphasis on sexual pleasure divorced from the context of a lifelong loving union, the comprehensive sex education favoured by the Sex Education Forum and its associated groups creates in young people the expectation that they will have a series of casual sexual relationships. As Hough remarks: 'It is no wonder that the hookup/friends-with-benefits/anything-goes sexual culture has become normalised among today's emerging adults.'[31] And within precisely that culture, child sexual exploitation has been allowed to go undetected, and vulnerable young people have found themselves without the protection they need.

30 Cassandra Hough, *op. cit.*

31 *Ibid.*

CHAPTER 16

The sexual 'rights' of children and young people

'With an enhanced understanding of young people, autonomy and sexual rights, we hope to be better placed to promote and fulfil our vision of a world where young people are recognised as rights-holders, decision-makers and sexual beings whose contributions, opinions and thoughts are valued equally, particularly in relation to their own sexual and reproductive health and well-being.'[1]

In our examination of the factors that have contributed to the normalisation of underage sex, we have maintained a focus on developments in the UK. However, the changing social attitudes and policies that we have considered cannot be fully understood without seeing them in the context of an international movement to promote the 'sexual rights' of children and young people.

The International Planned Parenthood Federation (IPPF) is a worldwide movement consisting of 152 member associations from different parts of the world. Registered as a charity in the UK and based in London, IPPF's vision is for a world in which 'all people are free to make choices about their sexuality and wellbeing'. In its policy on 'Meeting the Sexual and Reproductive Health Rights of Young People', the Federation states its commitment to 'working for and with young people to ensure that they are supported and empowered in their decisions relating to sex and sexuality'. Defining 'adolescence' as 10-19 years and 'young people' as 10-24 years, the policy 'acknowledges the right of all young people to enjoy sex and express their sexuality in the way that they choose'.[2]

The policy on the rights of young people goes on to state IPPF's 'commitment to work towards removing all social, legal, administrative

1 Ester McGeeney and Simon Blake, *Understanding young people's right to decide: 5. How do we assess the capacity of young people to make autonomous decisions?* IPPF, 2012.

2 IPPF, 'Meeting the Sexual and Reproductive Health Rights of Young People', Policy 4.7, included in IPPF, *Policy Handbook*, November 2014.

and institutional barriers that adversely affect young people's sexual and reproductive rights'. It also supports the provision of 'comprehensive sexuality education' that 'helps young people acquire the skills to negotiate relationships and safer sexual practices, including whether and when to engage in sexual intercourse' and that equips them with 'the knowledge, skills, attitudes and values they need to determine and enjoy their sexuality'.[3]

Sexuality education as 'a need and entitlement'

In June 2009, UNESCO (United Nations Educational Scientific and Cultural Organisation) issued *International Guidelines on Sexuality Education.* Sub-titled 'An evidence informed approach to effective sex, relationships and HIV/STI education', the guidance described sexuality education as a 'need and entitlement' of all children from the age of five. This right places upon education and health authorities and institutions an obligation to deliver sex education as part of their 'duty of care'.[4]

The 98-page document set out the various elements that should be included within a programme of sexuality education under different age categories. Among the 'key ideas' to be communicated to children aged 5-8, the guidance includes:

- Difference between consensual sexual activity and forced sex
- Girls and boys have private body parts that can feel pleasurable when touched by oneself
- It is natural to explore and touch parts of one's own body
- Touching and rubbing one's genitals is called masturbation
- Masturbation is not harmful, but should be done in private.[5]

At ages 9-12, children are to be given 'a broad, rights-based approach to sexuality education' which will include:

- Specific steps involved in obtaining and using condoms and contraception, including emergency contraception
- Specific means of preventing unintended pregnancy
- Correct and consistent use of condoms and contraception to prevent

3 *Ibid.*

4 UNESCO, *International Guidelines on Sexuality Education: An evidence informed approach to effective sex, relationships and HIV/STI education*, June 2009, pp.2-3.

5 *Ibid.*, pp. 42, 43, 48.

pregnancy, HIV and other STIs
- Relationship between excitement and vaginal lubrication, penile erection and ejaculation
- Masturbation is often a person's first experience of sexual pleasure
- Definition and function of orgasm
- Concept, examples and positive and negative effects of 'aphrodisiacs'
- Options available to teenagers who are unintentionally pregnant
- Definition of abortion
- Legal abortion performed under sterile conditions by medically trained personnel is safe.[6]

In any other context, the provision of such information is likely to be viewed as a form of grooming. But there is more, because at ages 12-15, pupils progress to learning, among other things:

- If sexual *(sic)* active, using communication skills to practice safe and consensual sex
- Respect for the different sexual orientations and gender identity
- Masturbation is a safe and valid expression of sexuality
- Contraceptives and condoms give people the opportunity to enjoy their sexuality without unintended consequences
- Both men and women can give and receive sexual pleasure with a partner of the same or opposite sex
- Regardless of their marital status, sexually active young people have the right to access contraceptives and condoms
- Obtaining and using condoms and contraceptives (including emergency contraception where legal and available)
- Overcoming barriers to obtaining and using condoms and contraception
- Identify local sources of condoms and contraceptives
- Use and misuse of emergency contraception
- Access to safe abortion and post-abortion care
- People living with HIV have a right to sexuality education and to express their love and feelings via sexuality.[7]

---

6 *Ibid.*, pp. 38, 44, 48, 49, 51.
7 *Ibid.*, pp. 37, 48, 50, 52, 55.

The agenda to change social norms

The guidelines state that the learning objectives do not represent an exhaustive list, but are rather part of 'a basic minimum package' that should feature in a comprehensive sexuality education programme. According to the document, the aim is not limited to teaching children and young people what they 'need to know' but also includes what they 'are curious about'.[8]

In a remarkably candid section, the guidelines admit that 'only some of these learning objectives are specifically designed to reduce risky sexual behaviour' and that there is a much more wide-reaching agenda in operation. 'Most' of the sexuality education learning objectives are intended 'to change social norms, facilitate communication of sexual issues, remove social and attitudinal barriers and increase knowledge'.[9]

The framers of the guidelines are fully aware of the fact that many politicians, policymakers and parents will be horrified at the thought of such an explicit approach to sex education. In order to 'minimise opposition', they recommend holding discussions 'at and across all levels' to 'desensitise' the critics, and are particularly concerned to win over the teaching profession:

> Teachers responsible for the delivery of sexuality education will usually also need desensitisation and training in the use of active, participatory learning methods.[10]

Although the *International Guidelines on Sexuality Education* are not legally binding, government-funded organisations in the UK such as Brook and the UK's IPPF-affiliate, the *fpa*, are promoting precisely this approach through one-to-one contact with young people and through sex education materials in schools and other youth settings. While the guidelines do not currently appear on the UNESCO website, they remain available on the UNHCR website and continue to be cited by the Department for Education[11] and by organisations such as the Sex Education Forum[12] and the Terrence Higgins Trust.[13]

---

8 *Ibid.*, p.26.

9 *Ibid.*

10 *Ibid.*, p.10.

11 Department for Education, *Personal, social, health and economic (PSHE) education: a review of impact and effective practice*, March 2015.

12 Sex Education Forum, Written evidence to the Culture, Media and Sport Committee, September 2013.

13 Terrence Higgins Trust, Written submission to the Inquiry into Personal, Social, Health and Economic

Young people as sexual 'rights-holders'

In the introduction to a document on assessing the capacity of young people to make autonomous decisions, the IPPF describes its mission in terms of

> work[ing] towards a world where women, men and young people everywhere have control over their own bodies, and therefore their destinies. We defend the right of all young people to enjoy their sexuality free from ill-health, unwanted pregnancy, violence and discrimination.[14]

It continues in the same vein to spell out the 'rights' of young people:

> IPPF believes that all young people have the right to make autonomous decisions about their sexual and reproductive health in line with their evolving capacities...
>
> One such barrier that impedes young people's access to education and services is the widely-held and historically-rooted belief that young people are incapable of making positive decisions about their own sexual and reproductive health...
>
> With an enhanced understanding of young people, autonomy and sexual rights, we hope to be better placed to promote and fulfil our vision of a world where young people are recognised as rights-holders, decision-makers and sexual beings whose contributions, opinions and thoughts are valued equally, particularly in relation to their own sexual and reproductive health and well-being.[15]

Written by two British authors, Ester McGeeney and the then chief executive of Brook, Simon Blake, the document welcomes the legal and policy framework in the UK, which, it says, 'is broadly supportive of young people's sexual rights and provides a favourable administrative context within which to support the development of young people's sexual autonomy'. It particularly applauds confidential sexual health services offering young people access to contraception and abortion.[16]

The document favours 'rights-based approaches that take account of young people's needs and interests and that affirm young people's right to experience pleasure and choice in their sexual identity and practices'.

---

education and Sex and Relationships Education in schools, June 2014.

14 Ester McGeeney and Simon Blake, *Understanding young people's right to decide*, op. cit.

15 *Ibid.*

16 *Ibid.*, p.2.

Such an approach, it maintains, is consistent with the principles outlined in the United Nations Convention on the Rights of the Child, and with the World Health Organisation's definition of sexual health.[17]

The impression is given that sexual pleasure and enjoyment is a 'right' and a 'choice' that can be freely exercised regardless of age.

The only reference to the age of consent in the entire paper appears in connection with the equalisation of the age of consent between homosexual and heterosexual young people and between the different countries within the UK. Other than that, the impression is given that sexual pleasure and enjoyment is a 'right' and a 'choice' that can be freely exercised regardless of age. Indeed, we are told that 'comprehensive sexuality education' is necessary '[i]n order to support the development of young people's capacity to make decisions and affirm their right to make choices about when and where they have sex, and what kind of sex they have'.[18]

The right of young people to sexual pleasure features prominently in the document. It commends the Sheffield Centre for HIV and Sexual Health for its training courses for professionals on 'how to include pleasure messages in sexual health work with young people' and for its pamphlet for professionals and parents on 'how and why to raise the issue of sexual pleasure with young people'.[19] With specific reference to the *Pleasure* leaflet, the IPPF document asserts that:

> In this resource and in the academic literature it is suggested that communicating to young people their right to pleasure and what they can gain from safer and consensual sexual practices will help to decrease the potential for regret, coercion and unsafe sexual practices and increase young people's capacity for autonomy and agency.[20]

The path to children's sexual liberation

There is nothing particularly new about this emphasis on the sexual rights of children and young people. In 1978, a World Health Organisation

17 *Ibid.*, p.7.
18 *Ibid.*, p.8.
19 *Ibid.*, p.8. This is a reference to the leaflet entitled *Pleasure*, discussed in chapter 15.
20 *Ibid.*

working party on young people aged 14-18 expressed the desire that sex education would enable teenagers to have 'positive and constructive' sexual experiences:

> While induced abortion may be better than an unwanted child, contraception is better than an unwanted pregnancy and the best path to improved contraception is education for responsible behaviour. Increasing sexual activity among teens is a fact, and, rather than ignoring its existence or trying to stamp it out, it would seem more expedient to educate young people so that such an activity becomes a positive and constructive experience in the developmental process leading to responsible adulthood.[21]

Less than a decade later, Richard Ives, a former teacher and youth worker, contributed a chapter on children's sexual rights to a book on *The Rights of Children*. He argued that children possess at least three sexual rights: the right to freedom from sexual exploitation, the right to express their sexuality, and the right to sex education. He wrote:

> What is needed is less emphasis on the protection of children. Protection is very often translated and transformed by 'carers' and 'caring agencies' from meaning protection against others to protection from the child's own ideas and behaviour which are categorised as wayward or deviant. More emphasis is needed on the rights of children and young people to live their own lives as far as possible within the same boundaries which society sets for everyone else. For this to be realistic, two things must happen: the power of certain groups, in particular adult males and those who care for children (parents, teachers, social workers etc), will have to be curtailed, and children must be enabled, by education and training as much as anything, to cope with the greater complexities of their liberated life.[22]

This 'liberated life' includes liberation from the authority and supervision of their parents. Such were the sentiments expressed by Nathalie Lieven, counsel for the *fpa*, in her defence of confidential sexual health services in a judicial review hearing in 2005. Ms Lieven told the High Court that the view that parents know what is best for a child is out of date and represents a traditional paternalistic approach that is out of

21 Cited by Richard Ives, 'Children's Sexual Rights' in Bob Franklin (ed), *The Rights of Children*, Blackwell, 1986, p.159.
22 *Ibid*, p.157.

step with recent social changes. She declared, 'Children have autonomous rights that must be protected by the courts.'

> *A requirement on professionals to report a young person for underage sexual activity 'could be considered an invasion of the young person's right to private life'.*
> Office of the Children's Commissioner for England

She further argued that parents are no longer necessarily the best people to advise a child on contraception, sexually transmitted infections and abortions, and that they have no right to know if their children under 16 are seeking treatment. She expressed particular concern about the influence of parents who had 'strong views' about underage sex, abortion, or teenagers having babies, and held that there was no reason why parents should know if their children did not wish to tell them. The autonomy of the child needed to be respected, and in the event of any clash between the right of the parent and the right of the child, 'the child's right must prevail', she insisted.

It was on the same basis that the Office of the Children's Commissioner for England opposed the mandatory reporting of sexual activity involving children under the age of 13. A paper prepared by Professor Carolyn Hamilton of the Children's Legal Centre on behalf of the commissioner suggested that a requirement on professionals to report a young person for underage sexual activity 'could be considered an invasion of the young person's right to private life'. The paper went on to oppose mandatory reporting of sexually active under 13s on the basis that children under that age who were being abused would not seek contraception or confide in a professional if they thought they would be reported.[23] In his annual report, the children's commissioner subsequently stated that 'opposing mandatory reporting of sexual activity in under-13s' fulfilled the *Every Child Matters* objectives to 'Be healthy' and 'Stay safe'.[24]

In the name of the sexual rights of children, the law on the age of consent has been watered down, contraceptive advice and treatment is being supplied to young teenagers in confidence in line with government guidance and professional protocols, and, as we shall see in the next chapter, a widely-used 'safeguarding tool' regards unlawful consensual

23 Response of the Office of the Commissioner for Children to 'Working with sexually active people under the age of 18 – a pan-London protocol'.

24 Office of the Children's Commissioner, *Annual Report 2005/06*.

sex worthy of 'positive feedback'. Meanwhile sex education in many schools is being delivered in a moral vacuum, with pupils told that only they can decide when and with whom to have sex, and that, provided it is consensual and preferably with contraception, there is nothing wrong with it.

In such a climate, it comes as no surprise when professionals charged with protecting children from sexual abuse view underage sexual activity with complacency and fail to take action. Not only is children's rights ideology undermining the responsibilities of parents for the care and protection of their children, but it is also undermining the basic principles of child protection.

CHAPTER 17
The Brook Sexual Behaviours Traffic Light Tool

'Our highly acclaimed Sexual Behaviours Traffic Light Tool supports professionals working with children and young people by helping them to identify and respond appropriately to sexual behaviours…

'By categorising sexual behaviours as green, amber or red, professionals across different agencies can work to the same standardised criteria when making decisions and can protect children and young people with a unified approach.

'Professionals who work with children and young people have told us they often struggle to identify which sexual behaviours are potentially harmful and which represent healthy sexual development. This is why it is vital that professionals agree on how behaviours should be categorised regardless of culture, faith, beliefs, and their own experiences or values.'[1]

The Brook traffic light tool is a resource designed to help professionals:

- make decisions about safeguarding children and young people;
- assess and respond appropriately to sexual behaviour in children and young people; and
- understand healthy sexual development and distinguish it from harmful behaviour.[2]

The tool lists a variety of sexual behaviours and categorises them as 'green', 'amber' or 'red' by age category, depending on whether the behaviour is to be encouraged, regarded as a matter of potential concern, or treated as unsafe and unhealthy.

It was originally developed by Family Planning Queensland in Australia, but adapted for use in the UK with funding from the

1 Brook, Sexual Behaviours Traffic Light Tool. *https://www.brook.org.uk/our-work/category/sexual-behaviours-traffic-light-tool* Accessed 16 February 2017.

2 Brook, Guidance for using the sexual behaviours traffic light tool, October 2014.

Department for Education. In addition to Brook employees from different parts of the country, the 19-strong advisory group included representatives from the NSPCC, the Royal College of General Practitioners, the British Youth Council and Stonewall.[3]

> *The Brook Traffic Light Tool gives the green light to 'consenting oral and/or penetrative sex with others of the same or opposite gender who are of similar age and developmental ability', aged 13-17.*

The traffic light tool is intended to show professionals working with children and young people 'which behaviours are a natural part of growing up and exploring sexuality, and which are problematic and may need intervention or support'. The stated aim is to provide 'a standardised normative list' to create 'a unified approach to protecting children and young people'.[4]

Giving a green light to underage sex

According to the tool, sex involving 13-17 year-olds should be viewed in a favourable light, provided it is consensual and 'between children or young people of similar age or developmental ability'. The green light is accordingly given to:

> consenting oral and/or penetrative sex with others of the same or opposite gender who are of similar age and developmental ability.

This is deemed 'reflective of natural curiosity, experimentation, consensual activities and positive choices'. Brook adds: 'Green behaviours provide opportunities to give positive feedback and additional information.'[5]

Other 'green behaviours' considered worthy of 'positive feedback' to 13-17 year-olds include 'solitary masturbation', 'sexually explicit conversations with peers' and 'interest in erotica/pornography', all of which are placed on the same level as 'choosing not to be sexually active'.[6]

The Brook traffic light tool with its relaxed approach to underage

3 Brook, Background to the traffic light tool, *https://www.brook.org.uk/our-work/background-to-the-traffic-light-tool* Accessed 16 February 2017.

4 Brook, Guidance for using the sexual behaviours traffic light tool, *op. cit.*

5 *Ibid.*

6 *Ibid.*

consensual sexual activity is widely used by professionals in a range of spheres, including teachers, social workers, school nurses, youth workers and police officers. According to Brook, the traffic light tool is being actively promoted as an important safeguarding tool by the NSPCC, Barnardo's, the Royal College of General Practitioners, the National Policing Improvement Agency, Local Safeguarding Children Boards, the Who Cares? Trust, Family Lives, Stonewall, the British Youth Council, the University of Sheffield, PSHE Association, the Youth Offending Service, CEOP and The Havens.[7]

In March 2014, Cornwall County Council became the first local authority to formally adopt the traffic light tool,[8] and it has been endorsed and promoted by numerous safeguarding children boards throughout the country.[9] Hertfordshire County Council 'recommends that education settings use The Sexual Behaviours Traffic Light Tool by the Brook Advisory Service to help professionals assess and respond appropriately to sexualised behaviour',[10] and the resource features prominently in the authority's risk assessment management plan.[11] The tool is also signposted in school safeguarding and child protection policies in other regions.[12]

A widely-used 'safeguarding tool'

The traffic light tool is warmly commended in numerous documents intended for the use of child protection professionals. For example, a national proforma for identifying risk of child sexual exploitation in sexual health services produced by the British Association for Sexual Health and HIV (BASHH) in association with Brook, signposts the tool and states that, 'It is important to understand CSE in the context that most

7 Brook, Further written evidence submitted to the House of Commons Education Committee, November 2014, Ref SRE0469.

8 Healthy Schools Cornwall, 'The new Sexual Behaviours Traffic Light Tool will be formally launched at Truro's Health and Wellbeing Innovation Centre on Tuesday 4 March', 1 March 2014.

9 For example, Norfolk Safeguarding Children Board, Letter to headteachers on ' Tackling Child Sexual Abuse in Norfolk - Call to Action', 1 July 2016; Staffordshire Safeguarding Children Board and Stoke-on-Trent Safeguarding Children Board, Inter-Agency Procedures for Safeguarding Children and Promoting their Welfare, April 2015; Wirral Local Safeguarding Children Board, Procedures Manual, Section 4.3 'Children and Young People who Display Sexually Inappropriate and Harmful Behaviour'.

10 Frazer Smith, *Model Child Protection Policy for Schools*, Hertfordshire County Council Children's Services, September 2016.

11 Hertfordshire Children's Services, *Guidance on the evaluation and management of child sexual behaviour*, March 2016.

12 To take just two examples, Muswell Hill Primary School, Child Protection Policy, September 2015, and St Helen's Catholic Primary School, Southend, Safeguarding and Child Protection Policy, December 2015.

sexual behaviour among young people is part of normal development.'[13]

Primarily intended as a guide for professionals working with young people under 18, the proforma was funded by the Department of Health and is endorsed by a number of professional bodies, including the Faculty of Sexual and Reproductive Healthcare, the Metropolitan Police, the National Pharmacy Association, Public Health England, the Royal College of Paediatrics and Child Health, and the Royal College of Physicians. It is used in most genitourinary medicine (GUM) clinics.

When Brook collaborated with the Sex Education Forum and the PSHE Association to produce advice on sex and relationships education to supplement the Department for Education guidance published in 2000, it was only to be expected that the new document would include the traffic light tool in a list of 'useful resources'. It recommends the Brook tool as an aid 'to help teachers develop lessons that will teach young people to recognise the signs of exploitation or abuse, and to seek help if it happens to them or someone they know'. It adds that the traffic light tool is designed 'to help professionals assess whether children and young people's sexual behaviours are healthy or unhealthy'.[14] This supplementary advice has been warmly welcomed and commended by government ministers and the Department for Education.

Schools Minister, Nick Gibb, described the guidance as 'very high quality' and 'carefully and sensitively worded'. He said that his department would be directing schools to the document 'because these are the experts in the field'. Referring to Brook, the Sex Education Forum and the PSHE Association, the minister added:

> The approach we are taking is that we will point schools and teachers to respectable organisations in this country that have a good reputation as being the people who produce the resources that schools need, as we do in maths and French, and so on.[15]

Multi-agency teams in some parts of the country have adopted the traffic light tool in their work. For example, the Sheffield Youth Justice

13 Karen Rogstad and Georgia Johnston, *Spotting the Signs: a national proforma for identifying risk of child sexual exploitation in sexual health services*, BASHH and Brook, 2014, p.16.

14 Brook, PSHE Association, Sex Education Forum, *Sex and Relationships Education (SRE) for the 21st Century*, op. cit., p.10.

15 Nick Gibb, Minister of State for Schools, in oral evidence presented to the House of Commons Education Committee, 17 December 2014.

Service is committed to training relevant professionals from its four statutory partnering organisations to use the Brook resource.[16]

Other bodies and organisations which commend the traffic light tool as a safeguarding resource include the National Institute for Health and Care Excellence (NICE),[17] the Royal College of General Practitioners (RCGP),[18] the NSPCC,[19] and Barnardo's.[20]

Responding to criticism

The traffic light tool has not been without controversy. It attracted considerable press attention in November 2014 after Sarah Carter of the Family Education Trust had referred to it in oral evidence before the House of Commons Education Committee. Mrs Carter expressed concern that a tool which presents sexual activity at the age of 13 as part of normal behaviour and development is informing the judgment of teachers and other professionals working with children and young people with regard to safeguarding issues. In response to press reports that were critical of the traffic light tool, Brook issued a statement insisting that:

> The Sexual Behaviours Traffic Light Tool is evidence-based, developed by experts. It is supported by the people and organisations who know most about healthy and non-healthy sexual development in the UK. It does not condone or encourage particular behaviours, nor is it about the law relating to sexual behaviour.[21]

However, it is difficult to see how giving positive feedback to sexually active children aged 13, 14 and 15 does not constitute condoning and encouraging underage sex. The press statement went on to argue that: 'It is clear professionals must use the tool "within the context of their own policies, legal frameworks and competencies".'

While it is true that Brook's guidance for using the Sexual Behaviours

16 Sheffield Youth Justice Service, 'Sheffield's Multi-Agency Work with Young People with Harmful Sexual Behaviour'. *http://www.safeguardingsheffieldchildren.org.uk*. The partners involved are the police, probation, health and children, young people and families services.

17 NICE, *Harmful sexual behaviour among children and young people*, NICE Guideline, NG55, 20 September 2016.

18 RCGP and NSPCC, *Safeguarding Children and Young People: The RCGP/NSPCC Safeguarding Children Toolkit for General Practice*, August 2014.

19 S Hackett, D Holmes and P Branigan, *Operational framework for children and young people displaying harmful sexual behaviours*, NSPCC, 2016.

20 Ghani, *Now I know it was wrong*, op. cit.

21 Brook statement on the Sexual Behaviours Traffic Light Tool, 5 November 2014.

Traffic Light Tool does include this proviso, the fact remains that professionals are not at liberty to create their own law on the age of consent. The law is clear: sex under the age of 16 is unlawful. To give it the green light and to reward it with positive feedback is to treat the law with contempt and to encourage lawbreaking. Yet this tool is currently informing the judgment of tens of thousands of teachers and other professionals working with children and young people with regard to safeguarding issues.

In giving 'positive feedback' to underage sexual relationships deemed to be consensual, professionals may inadvertently be condoning and promoting sexual exploitation and abuse.

There is a very real danger that the Brook traffic light tool will further encourage a climate in which underage sex is seen as a normal part of growing up. Where that happens, professionals can all too easily become oblivious to abuse and exploitation. In Liverpool, Child D was regarded 'as an adult making her own choices'.[22] Likewise, in Rochdale, professionals failed to intervene to protect teenage girls from abuse because they 'simply assumed that the young people were making a "lifestyle choice".'[23] Similarly, in Rotherham, 'children as young as 11 were deemed to be having consensual sexual intercourse when in fact they were being raped and abused by adults'.[24] Meanwhile, in Bristol, an investigating police officer told the parent of a girl who had been raped twice that the girl was 'making lifestyle choices'.[25] In giving 'positive feedback' to underage sexual relationships deemed to be consensual, professionals may inadvertently be condoning and promoting sexual exploitation and abuse.

22 Liverpool Safeguarding Children Board, *Overview Report*, op. cit., para 1.2.33.

23 *Rochdale 1-6*, op. cit., para 4.3.21.

24 Jay, *Independent Inquiry*, op. cit., para 8.1.

25 Myers and Carmi, *The Brooke Serious Case Review*, op. cit., para 7.2.7.

PART 3
CONCLUSION AND RECOMMENDATIONS

'[I]f under-age sex no longer feels illegal to those who are under-age, then you can bet that it will matter less and less to predatory adults as well. In Britain we have abandoned innumerable young girls to a host of risky situations, ranging from the regrettable to the life-destroying.'[1]

In Part Two, we highlighted a number of factors which have contributed to the repeated failure of child protection and law-enforcement agencies to recognise horrific cases of child sexual exploitation in different parts of the country and to take necessary and decisive action.

Sexual activity under the age of 16 has become commonplace, in spite of the fact that it is unlawful. For decades, the law on the age of consent has been, at best, largely ignored, and, at worst, treated with contempt. If young people are aware of the law at all, they know that it is extremely unlikely to be enforced and so it has lost its power to restrain as much as it has been deprived of its capacity to protect.

On top of that, the confidential provision of contraception, sexual health advice and even abortions without reference to parents is sending out a powerful message that sexual activity under the age of 16 meets with the full approval of the health establishment. This same message is also being reinforced in many schools by the adoption of the amoral and relativistic approach to sex and relationships education favoured by organisations such as the Sex Education Forum, the PSHE Association, Brook and the *fpa*, and promoted by many local authorities.

Official guidance documents produced by professional bodies and governmental agencies are playing their part in condoning underage sexual activity by advising school nurses and GPs that under-16s have the same right to confidentiality in matters relating to contraception and sexual health as any other patient. The Brook traffic light tool, in

1 Jenny McCartney, 'Teenage girls suffer as we look the other way', *Sunday Telegraph*, 30 September 2012.

widespread use by professionals across a range of disciplines literally gives the green light to 'consenting oral and/or penetrative sex with others of the same or opposite gender who are of similar age and developmental ability'. As if that were not enough, the notion of 'the sexual rights of the child' is being communicated to many young people by direct or indirect means.

Yet the government has hitherto been strangely silent on any of these issues. Even though the normalisation of underage sex has been identified repeatedly in the serious case reviews as a reason for the complacency of child protection agencies, there is no indication of a desire to address these underlying issues either at the local or the national level.

In its consultation on 'Reporting and acting on child abuse and neglect', the government set out 'three clear objectives' in its 'comprehensive and wide ranging programme to tackle child sexual exploitation':

- **Tackling offending:** We will improve the ability of our government and law enforcement agencies to identify, pursue, investigate and prosecute offenders.
- **Reducing vulnerability:** We will identify and work to eliminate the conditions that give offenders the opportunity to commit child sexual exploitation.
- **Supporting victims and survivors:** We will support victims and survivors of child sexual exploitation.[2]

More recently, the government has published a progress report in which it claims to have delivered around 90 per cent of its commitments and achieved a step change in the response to child sexual exploitation. As one of the 'signs of success', it cites a 24 per cent increase in the recording of contact child abuse offences by the police. Over the next three years, the government pledges to concentrate its efforts on 'working hard before abuse takes place to deter potential offenders, as well as

2 HM Government, *Reporting and acting on child abuse and neglect*, July 2016, para 35.

improving resilience in children and young people'.[3]

A number of proposals are outlined in the progress report, but there is no indication that the government plans to act on the lessons in relation to the normalisation of underage sexual activity that flow eloquently and consistently from recent serious case reviews into episodes of child sexual exploitation. There is no suggestion that the government has any intention to get to the root of the matter and seek to effect change through practical actions such as conducting a review of the confidential provision of contraception to under-16s, or revising official guidance to professionals in the area of adolescent sexual behaviour.

The evidence supplied by the reports considered in Part One demonstrates the long overdue need for a review of professional attitudes towards underage sexual activity and an investigation into the unintended consequences of teenage pregnancy strategies which have a focus on sex education and the confidential provision of contraception, abortion and treatment for sexually transmitted infections.

In this concluding section, we shall return to the factors highlighted in Part Two and seek to chart a way forward by addressing the underlying cultural issues which have been neglected to date.

3 HM Government, *Tackling Child Sexual Exploitation: Progress Report*, February 2017.

CHAPTER 18

Recovering the age of consent

Prior to the latter years of the nineteenth century, girls aged 12 and above were able to legally consent to sexual intercourse. It was not until 1875 that the age of consent was raised to 13, and a decade later it was raised more substantially to 16 under the Criminal Law Amendment Act 1885 in order to protect children from abuse and exploitation.

While the age of consent for heterosexual sexual activity remains unchanged, its force has been substantially weakened by the introduction of CPS guidance stating that:

> Consensual sexual activity between, for example, a 14 or 15 year-old and a teenage partner would not normally require criminal proceedings in the absence of aggravating features...[1]

This guidance is based on the premise that there is a vast difference between an adult male engaging in sexual activity with a girl in her early teens, compared with that same girl engaging in sexual activity with a boyfriend of a similar age. On this basis it has been determined that the law should not ordinarily be enforced where two teenagers are engaging in consensual sex.

In short, the argument runs, while children need protection from predatory adults, they do not under normal circumstances require protection from each other. According to this perspective, consensual sexual activity between children under the age of 16 may be illegal, but it is harmless. Indeed, as we have seen, according to the Brook traffic light tool, it is not merely 'harmless': it is 'reflective of...positive choices' and provides an opportunity to give 'positive feedback'.[2]

1 Crown Prosecution Service, *Legal Guidance on Rape and Sexual Offences: Chapter 11.*
2 Brook Sexual Behaviours Traffic Light Tool, *op cit.*

Harmless activity?

It is the same kind of reasoning that has prompted a parliamentary inquiry to view sexting as a benign activity when conducted between children in a 'consensual relationship'. The inquiry's report states that:

> [I]t is important to emphasise that whilst sexting can constitute a criminal offence, it is not necessarily 'harmful sexual behaviour', in terms of being inappropriate to a child's age and development – for example such as when two teenagers of similar age in a consensual relationship exchange images of themselves.[3]

But are we justified in regarding sexting and consensual sexual activity among children as 'harmless'? Over recent years we have witnessed rising levels of sexually transmitted infections among young people[4] and mental health issues related to premature sexual activity.[5] Studies have shown high levels of subsequent regret among those who embarked on sexual relationships at an early age,[6] and statistics suggest that sexual experimentation among teenagers is not always as innocent as many are inclined to assume. A study undertaken by the NSPCC found that:

> 65.9 per cent of contact sexual abuse of children and young people (based on the reports of 0-17 years) was perpetrated by other children and young people under the age of 18 rather than by adults in or outside the home.[7]

This is without taking into account the effect that a complacent attitude towards underage sex has had upon child protection agencies in their handling of cases of child sexual exploitation. The evidence from the reports examined in Part One demonstrates that the current application of the law is failing to provide the protection that it was intended to give.

As Jennifer Davis has expressed it in her review of the work of the nineteenth century social reformer, Josephine Butler, when we water down the age of consent law, we 'blur the line between childhood and

---

3 Ghani, *Now I know it was wrong*, op. cit., p.21.

4 Public Health England, *Sexually transmitted infections and chlamydia screening in England, 2015*, Infection report, Vol 10, No 22, 11 October 2016.

5 D D Halfors *et al*, 'Adolescent depression and suicide risk: association with sex and drug behavior', *American Journal of Preventive Medicine*, Vol 27(3), October 2004, pp.224-31; Donald P Orr, Mary Beiter and Gary Ingersoll, 'Premature Sexual Activity as an Indicator of Psychosocial Risk', *Pediatrics*, Vol 87(2), February 1991.

6 A Osorio *et al*, 'First sexual intercourse and subsequent regret in three developing countries', *Journal of Adolescent Health*, Vol 50(3), March 2012, pp.271-8.

7 Lorraine Radford *et al*, *Child abuse and neglect in the UK today*, NSPCC, 2011, p.88.

adulthood, and prematurely hand young people over to the adult world of sex with all its attendant responsibilities and risks'.[8]

> When we water down the age of consent law, we blur the line between childhood and adulthood, and prematurely hand young people over to the adult world of sex with all its attendant responsibilities and risks.

Children and the law

Some have argued forcefully against the criminalisation of children for breaches of the Sexual Offences Act 2003. For example, in its position statement on Young People Who Post Self-Taken Indecent Images, the Association of Chief Police Officers (ACPO) stated:

> ACPO does not support the prosecution or criminalisation of children for taking indecent images of themselves and sharing them. Being prosecuted through the criminal justice system is likely to be distressing and upsetting for children, especially if they are convicted and punished. The label of 'sex offender' that would be applied to a child or young person convicted of such offences is regrettable, unjust and clearly detrimental to their future health and wellbeing.[9]

This statement has been superseded by a briefing note along similar lines produced by the College of Policing:

> In youth produced sexual imagery cases where there are no aggravating features, it may be appropriate to take an approach that is supportive of the children involved, rather than a criminal process. Decisions on the appropriate approach should be underpinned by careful assessment of the facts of the case: the presence of any aggravating features; the backgrounds of the children involved; and the views of significant stakeholders (such as parents/carers and the children's teachers).[10]

Where the making and sharing of youth produced sexual imagery

8 Jennifer Davis, *The age of consent: a warning from history: The work of Josephine Butler*, Christian Institute, 2009, p.20.

9 ACPO Child Protection and Abuse Investigation (CPAI) Group, ACPO CPAI Lead's Position on Young People Who Post Self-Taken Indecent Images, n.d., para 2.5.

10 College of Policing, *Briefing note: Police action in response to youth produced sexual imagery ('Sexting')*, November 2016, para 13. The briefing uses the term 'youth produced sexual imagery' to describe 'young people (under 18) sharing indecent images, stills or videos, of themselves or of others (i.e. of others under 18)'. The definition is intended to cover a range 'from consensual sharing to exploitation'.

'is considered non-abusive and there is **no evidence** of exploitation, grooming, profit motive, malicious intent...or it being persistent behaviour', outcome code 21 will be applied. Outcome code 21 states:

> 'Further investigation, resulting from the crime report, which could provide evidence sufficient to support formal action being taken against the suspect is not in the public interest – police decision.'[11]

It is difficult not to have some sympathy with these sentiments up to a point. However, we do not accept that the only alternative is to allow the present situation to continue. Turning a blind eye to the law on distributing, showing and making indecent images of children and to the law on the age of consent is placing children at risk.

As one commentator has written:

> Sending a sexually explicit image is an offence; call it 'sexting' and somehow it is not as serious, giving a potentially dangerous message to young girls (and boys) that indecent images of them are fair game, and passing them around for others to see is OK too. We must protect our young people by starting to see sexting as the crime it really is. It is not acceptable to break the law, and we should take the sending of explicit images as seriously as we do other crimes.[12]

Current guidance to schools states that, 'Whilst young people creating and sharing sexual imagery can be very risky, it is often the result of young people's natural curiosity about sex and their exploration of relationships.'[13] Therefore, schools are advised that there is usually no need to make a referral to the police '[i]f a young person has shared imagery consensually, such as when in a romantic relationship, or as a joke, and there is no intended malice'. However, 'a young person sharing someone else's imagery without consent and with malicious intent, should generally be referred to police and/or children's social care'.[14]

This ambivalence is placing headteachers in a very difficult position. Should they report 'youth produced sexual imagery' to the police or not? Rob Campbell, headmaster of Impington Village College, and a

---

11 *Ibid.*, paras 19-20 (emphasis in original).

12 Sarah Newton, 'Sexting is not a bit of harmless teenage fun – it's a crime, and it should be reported to police', *Independent*, 2 August 2016.

13 UK Council for Child Internet Safety, *Sexting in schools and colleges: Responding to incidents and safeguarding young people*, August 2016, p.8.

14 *Ibid.*, p.12.

member of the executive of the National Association of Head Teachers has commented:

> It's a very difficult decision to make — when has the line been crossed? If a 14-year-old is in a relationship and sends a scantily clad picture of herself to a boy, is that OK? If they then break up and he distributes it, it becomes revenge porn. If I don't report it, I might be enabling someone who then goes on to exploit girls.[15]

We can all agree that the harshest penalties and sanctions for sexual offences should be reserved for sexual predators who have abused and exploited children and young people. But that is not to say that children and young people should remain free to flout the law with complete impunity. The present arrangement whereby the CPS guidance nullifies the law for two children engaging in consensual sexual activity below the age of 16 effectively reduces the age of consent to 13. Even below the age of 13, there is often a disinclination to intervene. This makes a laughing-stock of the law and sends out all the wrong messages to children and young people about showing due respect for the rule of law.

While a single act of youthful sexual folly may not warrant a custodial sentence and an entry in the sex offenders' register, it should not be passed over with a nod and a wink. The children or young people concerned should be left in no doubt that they have committed a criminal offence and should receive a youth caution. Since youth cautions are customarily delivered at a police station in the presence of a parent or legal guardian, such a procedure would provide an opportunity for the police to impress upon those who bear the legal responsibility for the child that they have a crucial role to play in working to prevent any recurrence of the offence.

RECOMMENDATION 1

The CPS should review its guidance with a view to ensuring that due rigour is restored to the law on the age of consent. Revised guidance should ensure that consensual sex between children and young people under the age of 16 is not condoned and that appropriate action is taken to ensure that those who engage in underage sex are left in no doubt that they have committed a criminal offence and cautioned accordingly.

15 Javier Espinoza, '"Sexting" children should not be prosecuted, guidelines say', *Daily Telegraph*, 14 February 2016.

CHAPTER 19

Reconsidering the confidential provision of contraceptive advice and treatment to under-16s

The availability of contraceptive advice and treatment to children and young people below the age of consent is sending out the powerful message that underage sex meets with the approval of the health establishment. In addition, where such services are provided on school premises, pupils might be forgiven for concluding that the education establishment also fully endorses their sexual proclivities.

The fact that such services are invariably offered in confidence without any reference to the child's parent(s) reinforces the perception that the decision to become sexually active rests with the child, and the child alone. As the *Respect Yourself* website puts it:

> The only person who can tell you you're ready – is you – not your partner, not your folks not your friends and ultimately not a policeman.[1]

In response to growing concern about the sexual abuse of children during the early years of the twenty-first century, the government proposed legislation aimed at increasing the protection afforded to children. Among the new provisions was the creation of a new offence of 'arranging or facilitating commission of a child sex offence'.

Exemptions for sex educators and contraceptive providers

During the passage of the Sexual Offences Bill, organisations such as Brook and the *fpa* expressed concern that youth workers, school nurses and other health professionals who provided contraceptive advice to under-16s might be captured by the legislation and rendered liable to prosecution for 'arranging or facilitating commission of a child sex

1 Warwickshire County Council, op. cit., 'Sex and The Law'. *http://respectyourself.info/sex/sex-and-the-law* Accessed 17 February 2017.

offence'. They successfully pressed for an amendment to the Bill granting an exemption for sex educators and contraceptive providers. Section 14 of the resulting Sexual Offences Act 2003 accordingly states that a person does not commit an offence but 'acts for the protection of a child if he acts for the purpose of':

> (a) protecting the child from sexually transmitted infection,
>
> (b) protecting the physical safety of the child,
>
> (c) preventing the child from becoming pregnant, or
>
> (d) promoting the child's emotional well-being by the giving of advice.

The CPS explains:

> This means that parents, doctors, other health professionals, in fact anyone can provide sexual health advice to children as long as their only motivation in doing so is the protection of the child.[2]

The suggestion that confidential contraceptive and sexual health services encourage underage sexual activity and fuel the flames of promiscuity is vehemently denied by service providers. It is claimed rather that such clinics are providing a valuable and necessary service to children and young people who are going to engage in sexual activity come what may. If such services were to be withdrawn, it is argued, there would be a marked increase in under-16 conception rates.

However, the evidence does not bear out this contention. Between December 1984, when the Court of Appeal ruled in favour of Victoria Gillick, and October 1985, when the House of Lords overturned the Court's decision, there was a period of almost a year during which contraceptive advice could not legally be given to girls under the age of 16 without parental consent. While attendances by under-16s at family planning clinics decreased by over 30 per cent during those 10 months, the under-16 conception rate remained unchanged (Figure 1). In his analysis of the statistics, Professor David Paton of Nottingham University Business School found no evidence that the Court of Appeal ruling in favour of Mrs Gillick led to an increase in either underage conception or abortion rates.[3]

2 Crown Prosecution Service, *Factsheet on Sexual Offences*, op. cit.

3 David Paton, 'The economics of family planning and underage conceptions', *Journal of Health Economics* 21 (2002) pp.207-225.

Figure 1: Rates of under-16 conceptions and attendances at family planning clinics, England 1980–1990

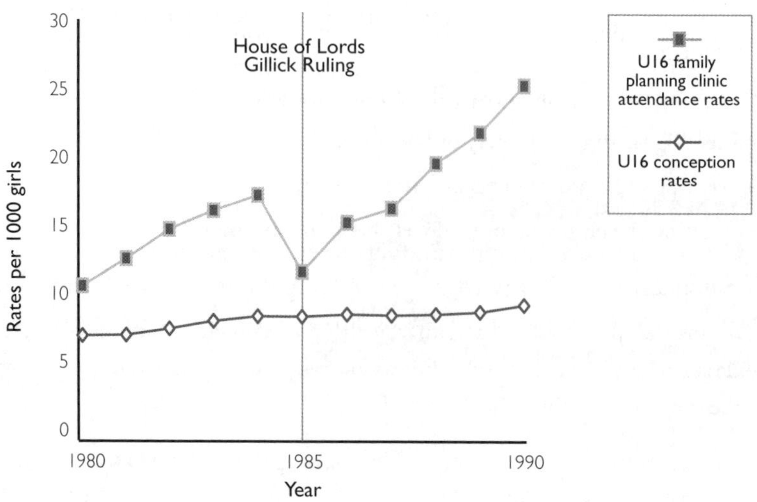

Sources: Teenage Pregnancy Unit and NHS, Contraceptive Services, England, various years

The following warning from the Oxfordshire serious case review merits careful attention:

> [T]he Review finds confusion related to a national culture where children are sexualised at an ever younger age and deemed able to consent to, say, contraception long before they are able legally to have sex. A professional tolerance to knowing young teenagers were having sex with adults seems to have developed.[4]

In addition to recovering the age of consent, if children and young people are to be afforded the protection they need, we shall need to reconsider the confidential provision of contraceptive advice and treatment for under-16s and review the terms of Section 14 of the Sexual Offences Act 2003.

4 Bedford, *Serious Case Review*, op. cit., para 1.3.

RECOMMENDATION 2

The Department of Health should review its guidance on the provision of advice and treatment to young people under 16 on contraception, sexual and reproductive health. Where sexually active young people under the age of consent are seeking advice in relation to contraception, sexually transmitted infections or abortion, there should be a requirement that their parent or legal guardian is notified.

RECOMMENDATION 3

Home Office ministers should conduct a review of Section 14 of the Sexual Offences Act 2003 with a view to removing the exemption for sex educators and contraceptive providers from charges of 'arranging or facilitating commission of a child sex offence'.

CHAPTER 20

Ensuring that all professional guidance pays due regard to the law on the age of consent

In keeping with the necessary revisions to the Department of Health guidance on the provision of advice and treatment to young people under 16 on contraception, sexual and reproductive health, amendments to other guidance for health professionals will be required.

RECOMMENDATION 4

The General Medical Council should amend its guidance for GPs to ensure that there is no further provision of contraceptive advice and treatment for children and young people under the age of 16.

RECOMMENDATION 5

The Department for Education, Department of Health and Public Health England should amend their guidance for school nurses and other health professionals to ensure that there is no further provision of contraceptive advice and treatment for children and young people under the age of 16.

CHAPTER 21

Restoring rigour and respect for parents in sex and relationships education

The law requires that where sex education is provided in a maintained school, the governing body and head teacher 'shall take such steps as are reasonably practicable to secure that…it is given in such a manner as to encourage those pupils to have due regard to moral considerations and the value of family life'.[1]

Also, the Secretary of State is required to issue guidance designed to ensure that pupils (a) 'learn the nature of marriage and its importance for family life and the bringing up of children', and (b) 'are protected from teaching and materials which are inappropriate having regard to [their] age and…religious and cultural background'.[2]

However, as we have seen, in practice many sex education programmes give little attention to moral considerations and the value of family life, marriage is frequently downplayed, and the explicit nature of some resources used has provoked alarm among parents. Advocates of sex education materials promoting relativism deny that such instruction sexualises children and insist that 'comprehensive sex and relationships education' delays sexual activity.

But any sex education programme which fails to place sexual intimacy within a clear and objective moral context will inevitably run the risk of encouraging underage sex. This is particularly true if a primary focus of the teaching is on the provision and use of contraception. Advice on how to engage 'safely' in an activity, coupled with provision to facilitate it, conveys the message that the activity itself is acceptable. One study found that 45.5 per cent of boys admitted that when they first received sex education, they felt the need to experiment. Considering that the majority of boys surveyed (77 per cent) had received sex education by the

1 Education Act 1996, s403(1).
2 Education Act 1996, s403(2).

age of 12, this is a particularly disturbing finding.[3]

Parents

While the current departmental guidance on sex and relationships education places a strong emphasis on consultation with parents and being sensitive to parental wishes and concerns, many schools have tended to exclude parents from policy development and merely inform them about decisions already made rather than positively engaging with them.

These trends have been given fresh impetus by the 'supplementary advice' on sex and relationships education, produced by the Sex Education Forum, PSHE Association and Brook, and promoted by the Department for Education. As noted earlier, the advice is devoid of references to morality, marriage and family life, plays down the role of parents and signposts the Brook traffic light tool.[4] Although it has no status in law, its promotion by education ministers and the Department for Education has helped to increase its influence.

Consent

Recent years have seen a growing emphasis on the need to teach about 'consent' in sex and relationships education lessons. As part of its strategy to prevent sexual violence, the government commissioned the PSHE Association to produce new guidance for teachers on teaching consent and has extended grant funding to the Association for it to continue advising schools, among other things, on 'teaching a better understanding of consent'.[5]

However, the PSHE Association's guidance to teachers on teaching consent offers no real clarity, but is rather a recipe for confusion. The guidance states:

> Despite what young people may feel in a given situation, there are legal boundaries to their ability to give consent, so any voluntary agreement to sexual activity by a child under 16 cannot be defined as consent in law. Below the age of consent, the law protects young people by prohibiting them from engaging in

3 Royal Forest of Dean College with Gloucestershire Community Health Council, *Sex Education & Family Planning Services Survey Results*, March 2000.

4 See Chapter 17.

5 HM Government, *Sexual violence and children and vulnerable people National Group: progress report and action plan* 2015, p.11.

> certain behaviours. It is important that young people fully understand these laws and recognise that they protect them from exploitation. However, **guidance from the Crown Prosecution Service** also states that, as long as neither partner is under 13, *'pupils of the same or similar age are highly unlikely to be prosecuted for engaging in sexual activity, where the activity is mutually agreed and there is no abuse or exploitation'.*[6]

Although the PSHE Association states that young people under the age of 16 lack the legal capacity to give consent to sexual activity, since consensual sexual activity between teenage peers is 'highly unlikely to be prosecuted', its guidance proceeds on the premise that under-16s can consent to sexual activity after all. In other words, it drives a wedge between 'consent in law' and consent in practice.

The lesson plan for a session on teaching 'consent and the law' accordingly begins:

> This lesson explores what consent means both legally and ethically. It is important to refer back to the section on consent and the law…, which states that the age of consent is 16 but that young people aged 13 to 15 are highly unlikely to be prosecuted for engaging in sexual activity with those of the same or similar age, if the activity is mutually agreed and there is no abuse or exploitation.[7]

The message being communicated to children and young people is: 'Although you can't legally give consent to sexual activity until you are 16, in practice you can, because it's extremely unlikely that you'll get into trouble for breaking the law.' Once again the law on the age of consent is being undermined and tacit approval is given of unlawful sexual activity.

The current emphasis on 'consent', as though it were the ultimate litmus test to determine whether or not sexual activity involving children and young people merits 'positive feedback' on the one hand or legal intervention on the other, is placing minors at risk of sexual exploitation. As the government's definition of child sexual exploitation acknowledges, a child or young person 'may have been sexually exploited even if the sexual activity appears consensual'.[8] The independent inquiry and serious case reviews studied in this report demonstrate over and over again that exploitative sexual activity has, at times, 'appeared consensual'

6 PSHE Association – *Teaching about consent*, op. cit., p.20 (emphasis in original).

7 *Ibid.*, p.29.

8 HM Government, *Definition of child sexual exploitation*, op. cit., p.3.

to both victims and professional onlookers alike. The evidence furnishes numerous examples of young people who believed themselves to be in a consensual relationship only to discover subsequently that they were being exploited. It also repeatedly highlights instances where professionals have made gross misjudgements about the nature of sexual activity involving minors and responded inappropriately on the false assumption that it was consensual.

Exploitative sexual activity has, at times, appeared consensual to both victims and professional onlookers alike.

RECOMMENDATION 6

The Department for Education should write to all schools, stressing the need to consult parents about their sex and relationships education provision, in line with current departmental guidance. Schools should be advised that they must uphold and teach the law on the age of consent and that they must not in any way condone sex under the age of 16. They must rather encourage pupils to have 'due regard to moral considerations and the value of family life' and teach 'the nature of marriage and its importance for family life and the bringing up of children'.

RECOMMENDATION 7

The Department for Education should review its decision to promote the supplementary advice produced by the Sex Education Forum, PSHE Association and Brook in view of its lack of regard for moral considerations, marriage and family life, its ambivalence towards parents and its endorsement of the Brook Sexual Behaviours Traffic Light Tool.

RECOMMENDATION 8

Sex and relationships education (and PSHE education of which it forms a part) should not be made a statutory part of the school curriculum. In view of the sensitive nature of the subjects involved, they should be viewed as the primary responsibility of parents. Schools should remain free to develop their own policies in relation to sex and relationships education in close consultation with parents, and primary school governing bodies should retain the discretion not to provide sex education. Also, parents should retain the legal right to withdraw their children from sex and relationships education lessons throughout their school career.

RECOMMENDATION 9

The Department for Education should not recommend the PSHE Association's guidance on the teaching of consent in schools in view of the mixed messages it communicates on the age of consent.

CHAPTER 22

Abolishing the notion of 'rights' in relation to the sexual activity of children and young people

In chapter 17, we considered how various national and international bodies are vigorously promoting the idea that children and young people have sexual 'rights'. Children are increasingly being viewed as autonomous individuals rather than members of a family. As a result of this trend, parental responsibilities are being usurped by those whose interest in children is professional rather than personal.

The family unit is the basic building-block that lies at the foundation of a stable society. We should therefore be wary of divorcing children from their parents in our thinking and policy-making. We should rather respect the role of parents as their children's primary providers, protectors and care-givers, and both permit and encourage them to fulfil their responsibilities.

RECOMMENDATION 10

The Department for Education and Department of Health should review all their guidance and other literature in relation to sex and relationships education and sexual health advice to ensure that it does not contain any suggestion that children and young people have a 'right' to sexual activity or to services designed to support sexual relationships under the age of 16.

RECOMMENDATION 11

All government departments and publicly-funded agencies should ensure that all guidance and policy documents relating to children and young people give explicit recognition to the role of parents (or legal guardians) as their children's primary providers, protectors, and care-givers. Children and young people should not be regarded and treated as autonomous individuals, but as members of a family.

CHAPTER 23

Discouraging the use of the Brook Sexual Behaviours Traffic Light Tool

In view of the findings of the serious case reviews highlighted in Part One, it is irresponsible, dangerous and an abdication of adult responsibility for teachers, health professionals and others to treat sexual activity below the age of consent as a 'positive choice' and an opportunity to give 'positive feedback'.

Any safeguarding tool which gives the green light to 'consenting oral and/or penetrative sex with others of the same or opposite gender who are of similar age and developmental ability', and regards 'sexually explicit conversations with peers' and 'interest in erotica/pornography' in a positive light is not fit for purpose.

RECOMMENDATION 12

The Department of Health, Department for Education, Home Office and any other government department or agency concerned with the protection of children and young people should ensure that the Brook Sexual Behaviours Traffic Light Tool is not recommended as a safeguarding tool in any of its guidance or training materials.

RECOMMENDATION 13

All government departments should ensure that any safeguarding tool, and any advice or guidance that they provide or signpost, places a strong emphasis on the age of consent and in no way communicates the message that sexual activity under the age of 16 is a legitimate choice worthy of positive feedback.

EPILOGUE

The serious case reviews and the Independent Inquiry into Child Sexual Exploitation in Rotherham considered in this report have highlighted social and cultural issues that cannot be resolved by improved communications or the restructuring of local authority or police departments. Unless we are prepared to address the root causes, we shall see more cases of child sexual exploitation.

There needs to be a fundamental change in how, as a society, we view children and young people, how we perceive parental responsibility, how we treat the family unit, and how we regard the law.

- If we continue to see young people as autonomous individuals with sexual 'rights', underage sex will continue to be normalised, children and young people will remain at increased risk, and child protection agencies will remain disinclined to intervene to protect them from abuse and exploitation.
- If we continue to view the sexual activity of children under the age of 16 as of no concern to their parents, we deprive children of the care and guidance of their foremost protectors and we shall make parents less inclined to take responsibility for them.
- If we treat the family unit as an irrelevance in the services we offer to children and young people, we are removing them from a vital accountability structure. We are also encouraging them to think and act in an individualistic way that will not help them to see the value of a supportive family network when they have children of their own.
- If we turn a blind eye to legal provisions intended for the protection of children and young people, we shall expose them to increased risk of abuse and teach them to treat the law with contempt.

For too long, we have failed to face up to these fundamental root issues. We cannot afford to turn a deaf ear and a blind eye to them any longer.

LIST OF RECOMMENDATIONS

Recommendation 1

The CPS should review its guidance with a view to ensuring that due rigour is restored to the law on the age of consent. Revised guidance should ensure that consensual sex between children and young people under the age of 16 is not condoned and that appropriate action is taken to ensure that those who engage in underage sex are left in no doubt that they have committed a criminal offence and cautioned accordingly.

Recommendation 2

The Department of Health should review its guidance on the provision of advice and treatment to young people under 16 on contraception, sexual and reproductive health. There should be no further provision of contraceptive advice to young people under the age of 16. Where sexually active young people under the age of consent are seeking advice in relation to sexually transmitted infections or abortion, there should be a requirement that their parent or legal guardian is notified.

Recommendation 3

Home Office ministers should conduct a review of Section 14 of the Sexual Offences Act 2003 with a view to removing the exemption for sex educators and contraceptive providers from charges of 'arranging or facilitating commission of a child sex offence'.

Recommendation 4

The General Medical Council should amend its guidance for GPs to ensure that there is no further provision of contraceptive advice and treatment for children and young people under the age of 16.

Recommendation 5

The Department for Education, Department of Health and Public Health England should amend their guidance for school nurses and other health professionals to ensure that there is no further provision of contraceptive advice and treatment for children and young people under the age of 16.

Recommendation 6

The Department for Education should write to all schools, stressing the need to consult parents about their sex and relationships education provision, in line with current departmental guidance. Schools should be advised that they must uphold and teach the law on the age of consent and that they must not in any way condone sex under the age of 16. They must rather encourage pupils to have 'due regard to moral considerations and the value of family life' and teach 'the nature of marriage and its importance for family life and the bringing up of children'.

Recommendation 7

The Department for Education should review its decision to promote the supplementary advice produced by the Sex Education Forum, PSHE Association and Brook in view of its lack of regard for moral considerations, marriage and family life, its ambivalence towards parents and its endorsement of the Brook Sexual Behaviours Traffic Light Tool.

Recommendation 8

Sex and relationships education (and PSHE education of which it forms a part) should not be made a statutory part of the school curriculum. In view of the sensitive nature of the subjects involved, they should be viewed as the primary responsibility of parents. Schools should remain free to develop their own policies in relation to sex and relationships education in close consultation with parents, and primary school governing bodies should retain the discretion not to provide sex education. Also, parents should retain the legal right to withdraw their children from sex education and relationships lessons throughout their school career.

Recommendation 9

The Department for Education should not recommend the PSHE Association's guidance on the teaching of consent in schools in view of the mixed messages it communicates on the age of consent.

Recommendation 10

The Department for Education and Department of Health should review all their guidance and other literature in relation to sex and relationships education and sexual health advice to ensure that it does not contain any suggestion that children and young people have a 'right' to sexual activity or to services designed to support sexual relationships under the age of 16.

Recommendation 11

All government departments and publicly-funded agencies should ensure that all guidance and policy documents relating to children and young people give explicit recognition to the role of parents (or legal guardians) as the primary providers, protectors, and care-givers of their children. Children and young people should not be regarded and treated as autonomous individuals, but as members of a family.

Recommendation 12

The Department of Health, Department for Education, Home Office and any other government department or agency concerned with the protection of children and young people should ensure that the Brook Sexual Behaviours Traffic Light Tool is not recommended as a safeguarding tool in any of its guidance or training materials.

Recommendation 13

All government departments should ensure that any safeguarding tool, and any advice or guidance that they provide or signpost, places a strong emphasis on the age of consent and in no way communicates the message that sexual activity under the age of 16 is a legitimate choice worthy of positive feedback.

INDEX